moroccan
cooking

FRAGRANTLY SPICED NORTH AFRICAN CUISINE

REBEKAH HASSAN

LORENZ BOOKS

This edition first published by Lorenz Books
an imprint of
Anness Publishing Limited
Hermes House
88–89 Blackfriars Road
London SE1 8HA

© 1997, 2000 Anness Publishing Limited

This edition distributed in Canada by, Raincoast Books
8680 Cambie Street, Vancouver, British Columbia V6P 6M9

ISBN 0-7548-0556-5

A CIP catalogue record for this book is available from the British Library

Publisher: Joanna Lorenz
Senior Cookery Editor: Linda Fraser
Copy Editor: Karen Douthwaite
Indexer: Hilary Bird
Designer: Ian Sandom
Photographer: William Lingwood, assisted by Louise Dare
Food for photography: Lucy McKelvie, assisted by Sophie Wheeler
Illustrator: Madeleine David

Front cover: William Lingwood, Photographer;
Helen Trent, Stylist; Sunil Vijayakar, Home Economist

Previously published as part of the *Creative Cooking Library*

Printed and bound in Hong Kong/China

1 3 5 7 9 10 8 6 4 2

MEASUREMENTS
For all recipes, quantities are given in both metric and imperial measures and,
where appropriate, measures are also given in standard cups and spoons. Follow
one set, but not a mixture because they are not interchangeable.

Standard spoon and cup measures are level
1 tsp = 5ml, 1 tbsp = 15ml, 1 cup = 250ml/8 fl oz

Medium eggs should be used unless otherwise stated.

CONTENTS

INTRODUCTION

For many people Moroccan food is an unknown quantity. There are few Moroccan restaurants outside Morocco and even in the country itself restaurants are a rare sight – good restaurants even rarer. Yet for those people who have had the pleasure of eating in Moroccan homes, or attending one of their grand and impressive banquets, Moroccan food is one of the country's unsung but undeniable delights. It may be one of the world's last undiscovered cuisines and, in terms of subtlety, delicacy, pure flavour and taste, can compare with the much more famous cuisines of France, India or China.

All great cuisines have evolved with thanks to influences from other lands. Morocco, looking one way to the Mediterranean and the other way to Africa, has been subject inevitably to a huge range of influences over the centuries, through trade as well as invasion.

The indigenous people of Morocco are the Berbers, a non-Arab race, who have inhabited North Africa since the earliest recorded time. They lived a simple rural life, tending crops and raising sheep and cattle, and even today many Berbers dwell in tents and clay huts in the foothills of the Atlas Mountains. The Berber influence on the cuisine of North Africa has been enormous. *M'choui*, whole lamb, rubbed with garlic and cumin and then roasted on a spit, is among the most famous Berber dishes and is still rightly enjoyed throughout the country, cooked and served in a manner that has not changed for centuries. Tagines, which are thick stews of meat and vegetables in rich gravy, are also well-known and popular Berber dishes and even *harira*, the thick soup of vegetables and pulses that has been adopted by Muslim Arabs as their traditional "break-fast" meal during Ramadan, was invented by the Berbers.

The most famous of all Berber dishes, however, is couscous – the national dish of Morocco. The word gives its name both to the dish itself and to the granules of semolina which form the basis of this speciality. These tiny pellets of grain, steamed above a tagine until tender, are piled into a pyramid and then covered with the rich meat and gravy of the tagine. It is a dish superb in its simplicity yet entirely unlike any other in the world and is one of the glories of Moroccan cuisine.

Berber is an almost completely spoken language, and recipes for couscous have been handed down by word of mouth to girls (it is always women in the kitchen in Morocco) by their mothers, aunts and grandmothers for literally centuries. Recipe books have never existed and even now are rare, yet there are hundreds of traditional couscous dishes and tagines and all Moroccan households have their own favourites.

The Arabs first invaded Morocco in 682, bringing with them an entirely different culture and religion – Islam. Food and the customs surrounding meals and eating were different too. Bread, which played – and still plays – an essential part in Arab life, was introduced to North Africa and was enthusiastically adopted and adapted, so that today it is one of the staple foods of

Left: A river provides the perfect wash basin for a farmer's fresh vegetables.

Bartering for goods (right) and a stall piled high with tagines (above) are common sights in a Moroccan marketplace.

Morocco. The Arabs, in their drive to expand the power of Islam, had reached out to countries and continents way beyond the experience of the Berbers. Persia, Syria and Egypt were conquered by the Muslim armies and in later centuries India, Indonesia and China came under their influence too. Consequently foods and dishes from the East were introduced into Moroccan culture. As is customary with food, people chose the bits they liked best – the ingredients that complemented their favourite dishes. Chick-peas and other pulses became popular, while spices, such as ginger, saffron, turmeric and – most important of all – cinnamon, became a central part of Moroccan cooking.

The Bedouins (whose name means dwellers of the desert) were nomadic Arabs who moved into Morocco from the 11th century onwards and they too had an influence on the country's food. Their diet included dates, milk and bread, while meat was roasted in pits or over wood fires out in the open.

The conquering Arabs made their way to Spain and, in turn, the influence of Spanish cuisine, partic-ularly of Andalucia, made its way back. Fruits like oranges, lemons and peaches were introduced, as were olives and olive oil. The Berbers had principally used *smen*, a type of preserved butter, for cooking, but olive oil was adopted, although traditional Berber dishes still use *smen* and it is a distinguishing feature of Berber cuisine today. Once trading routes are open, a huge dissemination of ideas and products takes place. New foods are naturally welcomed with interest and enthusiasm, and Morocco, like other Mediterranean countries, was quick to adopt tomatoes, peppers and other fruit and vegetables that the Spanish brought home from America. Paprika was introduced too and became hugely popular, especially in conjunction with cinnamon and ginger.

In the early 20th century, France and Spain ruled Morocco as a protectorate. Again, visitors to Morocco may notice occasional culinary influences – not so much in ingredients, but in the dishes themselves. Some salads have clearly been adapted from popular French ones and similarly Gazelles' Horns (*Kaab el Ghzal*), a traditional Moroccan dessert, has been adopted in France, where it is known as *cornes de gazelles*.

EATING MOROCCAN STYLE

Moroccan meals are usually served at low round tables. A simple meal might comprise one, or more often two, tagines, which are served with a selection of raw and cooked salads. However, for special occasions a couscous is frequently served, and for feasts and banquets it is essential. Bread is always served and a meal would be considered incomplete without it.

Finally, no book on Moroccan cooking would be complete without mention of the tea ceremony. Mint tea is as Moroccan as sunset over Marrakesh, and is wonderfully refreshing – far more so than any amount of fizzy drinks. Surprisingly, tea was introduced to Morocco as recently as the 1800s, but since then a ritual has evolved for making and drinking tea and it is served anywhere and everywhere, sipped for hours in cafés, in the home, or during endless bartering sessions in the medina.

INGREDIENTS

THE TEN ESSENTIALS

If you are planning to cook Moroccan food, you will find that some spices and herbs are called for again and again: they are the essence of the flavour of Morocco.

CINNAMON

Cinnamon is widely used in Moroccan cookery. It is added to soups and tagines, and fried pastries are commonly dusted with a mixture of ground cinnamon and sugar; Moroccans enjoy the distinctive fragrance, whether the filling is sweet or savoury. Cinnamon sticks give a more subtle flavour, but ground cinnamon is used more often.

CUMIN

Cumin is used frequently in soups and tagines and is especially popular in fish and poultry dishes. Grind the seeds in a pestle and mortar, or simply buy the spice ready-ground.

Below: Clockwise from the top: cumin seeds, saffron threads, cayenne pepper, ground turmeric, cinnamon sticks, ground cinnamon, paprika, black peppercorns, ground cumin and ground ginger (centre).

SAFFRON

Although a relatively expensive spice, small amounts of saffron are used extensively in Moroccan cookery, adding colour and a subtle aroma to dishes. The threads can be ground using a pestle and mortar or soaked to make saffron water.

TURMERIC

Although sometimes used instead of saffron, turmeric is also an important spice in its own right, adding colour and a characteristic pungency to soups. It is an essential ingredient in *harira*.

GINGER

This fragrant spice has a slightly hot, peppery taste. It is frequently used with paprika and black pepper, which contrast with its underlying sweetness. Ground ginger adds a more mellow flavour than the fresh root and is more commonly used by Moroccan cooks.

PAPRIKA

Paprika is hugely popular and used in numerous dishes. It is an essential element in *charmoula* and also is used in salads and tagines.

CAYENNE PEPPER

This fiery spice is popular in the more southern parts of Morocco, where food is more highly spiced.

BLACK PEPPER

Black pepper adds piquancy to many savoury dishes. Freshly grind black peppercorns rather than using ready-ground pepper.

Above: Flat leaf parsley (top) and fresh coriander (bottom) are used in large quantities in many Moroccan dishes.

PARSLEY

In Morocco, parsley is used far more as a vegetable than a herb, and while recipes here suggest moderate quantities, you could easily double the amount if liked. Moroccan cooks use flat leaf parsley, which has a mild, fragrant flavour, but curly leaf parsley can be used instead.

CORIANDER

Coriander is another essential ingredient in Moroccan cookery. It adds a wonderful pungency to dishes and, like parsley, is frequently used in large quantities. Pre-packed coriander is widely available in supermarkets, but if you have access to ethnic shops and markets, buy it in large bunches.

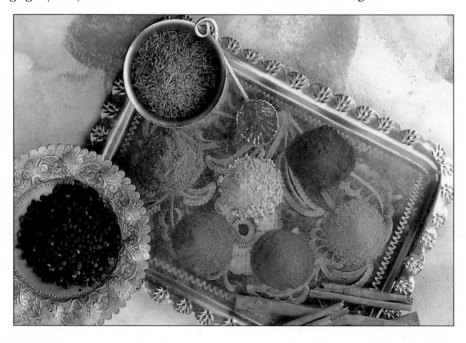

Clockwise from the top: Above: Blanched, whole, flaked and shelled almonds, dried chick-peas, couscous and ground almonds (centre). Right: Moroccan honey, black olives, tan olives, green olives, harissa, charmoula and preserved lemons.

OTHER INGREDIENTS

ALMONDS
Almonds are frequently used in Moroccan cooking. They can be blanched and used whole, chopped or flaked and then toasted and/or ground for fillings or stuffings.

CHARMOULA
Moroccan cooks almost always use this marinade when cooking fish. It usually includes garlic, cumin, paprika, cayenne pepper, fresh parsley and coriander, white wine vinegar, lemon juice and olive oil.

CHICK-PEAS
Chick-peas are extremely popular in Morocco, where they are used in soups, tagines and couscous dishes and are sold in the markets loose by the kilo; Moroccans would never use canned chick-peas. However, although the texture isn't the same, canned chick-peas can be used in place of fresh chick-peas.

COUSCOUS
Most of the couscous available in supermarkets is the precooked variety, which can be prepared quickly, by steaming, or soaking in boiling water or stock. Uncooked couscous is less easily available and is more complicated to cook, although the end result is good. Couscous may be cooked in a *couscousier*, a type of double saucepan in which a stew is simmered in the bottom half and the couscous is steamed in the top.

HARISSA
Occasionally, Moroccan dishes are spiced with harissa, a hot chilli paste from Algeria. If it is not available use Tabasco sauce instead.

HONEY
Moroccans have a very sweet tooth and use honey lavishly, not only in sweet dishes but in savoury ones as well. Moroccan honey is thick, with an aromatic, herbal flavour. Greek honey made from the nectar of thyme and rosemary flowers makes a good substitute.

OLIVES
There are three main types of Moroccan olives: unripe green olives, used mostly in salads; ripe, tan olives (which range in colour from deep green through rose and violet to dark red) and are the most popular; and black olives that have been cured in salt.

PRESERVED LEMONS
To make about 900g/2lb, quarter 5 lemons lengthways, to within 1cm/½in of the bottom. Weigh out 65g/2½oz salt. Sprinkle the lemon flesh with a little of the salt and reshape. Place 30ml/2 tbsp of the salt in a sterilized preserving jar and press in the lemons, sprinkling the remaining salt between the layers. Push down so that the lemons release their juice, then pour in enough lemon juice to cover the fruit completely. Leave for 20–30 days, shaking the jar every other day. When ready to use, remove as many lemons as required and rinse under running water. Remove and discard the pulp. Chop the skin finely or coarsely as required. Preserved lemons should keep for up to a year.

SOUPS AND STARTERS

Moroccans tend not to eat meals as we do in the West, with a soup
or starter, followed by a main course. Soup is normally eaten as a
supper dish and is a meal in itself. Harira is the famous soup eaten
by all Muslims after sundown during Ramadan, although
Moroccans enjoy it throughout the year. Appetizers, like Byesar and
Grilled Keftas, are usually eaten as snacks, but if you wish, serve
them either before or along with the main course.

Harira

Ingredients

Serves 6

75g/3oz/½ cup chick-peas, soaked
  overnight
15g/½ oz/1 tbsp butter
225g/8oz lamb, cut into cubes
1 onion, chopped
450g/1lb tomatoes, peeled
  and chopped
a few celery leaves, chopped
30ml/2 tbsp chopped fresh parsley
15ml/1 tbsp chopped fresh coriander
2.5ml/½ tsp ground ginger
2.5ml/½ tsp ground turmeric
5ml/1 tsp ground cinnamon
75g/3oz/scant ½ cup green lentils
75g/3oz vermicelli or soup pasta
2 egg yolks
juice of ½–1 lemon
salt and freshly ground black pepper
fresh coriander, to garnish
lemon wedges, to serve

1 Drain the chick-peas, rinse under cold water and set aside. Melt the butter in a large flameproof casserole or saucepan and fry the lamb and onion for 2–3 minutes, stirring, until the lamb is just browned.

2 Add the tomatoes, celery leaves, herbs and spices and season well with black pepper. Cook for about 1 minute and then stir in 1.75 litres/ 3 pints/7½ cups water and add the lentils and chick-peas.

3 Slowly bring to the boil and skim the surface to remove the surplus froth. Boil rapidly for 10 minutes, then reduce the heat and simmer very gently for about 2 hours or until the chick-peas are very tender. Season with salt and a little more pepper if necessary.

4 Add the vermicelli or soup pasta and cook for 5–6 minutes until it is just cooked through. If the soup is very thick at this stage, add a little more water.

5 Beat the egg yolks with the lemon juice and stir into the simmering soup. Immediately remove the soup from the heat and stir until thickened. Pour into warmed serving bowls and garnish with fresh coriander. Serve with lemon wedges.

> ──── Cook's Tip ────
>
> If you have forgotten to soak the chick-peas, place them in a pan with about four times their volume of cold water. Bring very slowly to the boil, and then cover and remove from the heat. Allow to stand for 45 minutes. They can then be drained and used as described in the recipe.

Chick-pea and Parsley Soup

INGREDIENTS

Serves 6

225g/8oz/1⅓ cups chick-peas, soaked
  overnight
1 small onion
1 bunch fresh parsley (about 40g/1½ oz)
30ml/2 tbsp olive and sunflower
  oil, mixed
1.2 litres/2 pints/5 cups chicken stock
juice of ½ lemon
salt and freshly ground black pepper
lemon wedges and finely pared strips of
  rind, to garnish
Moroccan bread, to serve

1 Drain the chick-peas and rinse under cold water. Cook them in boiling water for 1–1½ hours until tender. Drain and peel (see Cook's Tip).

2 Place the onion and parsley in a food processor or blender and process until finely chopped.

3 Heat the olive and sunflower oils in a saucepan or flameproof casserole and fry the onion mixture for about 4 minutes over a low heat until the onion is slightly softened.

4 Add the chick-peas, cook gently for 1–2 minutes and add the stock. Season well with salt and pepper. Bring the soup to the boil, then cover and simmer for 20 minutes until the chick-peas are very tender.

5 Allow the soup to cool a little and then part-purée in a food processor or blender, or by mashing the chick-peas fairly roughly with a fork, so that the soup is thick but still quite chunky.

--- COOK'S TIP ---

Chick-peas, particularly canned ones, blend better in soups and other dishes if the outer skin is rubbed away with your fingers. Although this will take you some time, the final result is much better, so it is well worth doing.

6 Return the soup to a clean pan, add the lemon juice and adjust the seasoning if necessary. Heat gently and then serve garnished with lemon wedges and finely pared rind, and accompanied by Moroccan bread.

Moroccan Vegetable Soup

Creamy parsnip and pumpkin give this soup a wonderfully rich texture.

INGREDIENTS

Serves 4
15ml/1 tbsp olive or sunflower oil
15g/½oz/1 tbsp butter
1 onion, chopped
225g/8oz carrots, chopped
225g/8oz parsnips, chopped
225g/8oz pumpkin
about 900ml/1½ pints/3¾ cups
   vegetable or chicken stock
lemon juice, to taste
salt and freshly ground black pepper

For the garnish
7.5ml/1½ tbsp olive oil
½ garlic clove, finely chopped
45ml/3 tbsp chopped fresh parsley and
   coriander mixed
good pinch of paprika

1 Heat the oil and butter in a large pan and fry the onion for about 3 minutes until softened, stirring occasionally. Add the carrots and parsnips, stir well, cover and cook over a gentle heat for a further 5 minutes.

2 Cut the pumpkin into chunks, discarding the skin and pith, and stir into the pan. Cover and cook for a further 5 minutes, then add the stock and seasoning and slowly bring to the boil. Cover and simmer very gently for 35–40 minutes until the vegetables are tender.

3 Allow the soup to cool slightly, then purée in a food processor or blender until smooth, adding a little extra water if necessary. Pour back into a clean pan and reheat gently.

4 To make the garnish, heat the oil in a small pan and gently fry the garlic and herbs for 1–2 minutes. Add the paprika and stir well.

5 Adjust the seasoning of the soup and stir in lemon juice to taste. Pour into warmed individual soup bowls and spoon a little garnish on top, which should then be carefully swirled into the soup.

Chicken Soup with Vermicelli

In Morocco, the cook – almost always a woman, often the most senior female of the household – would use a whole chicken for this nourishing soup, to serve her large extended family. This is a slightly simplified version, using chicken portions.

INGREDIENTS

Serves 4–6
30ml/2 tbsp sunflower oil
15g/½ oz/1 tbsp butter
1 onion, chopped
2 chicken legs or breast pieces,
    halved or quartered
flour, for dusting
2 carrots, cut into 4cm/1½ in pieces
1 parsnip, cut into 4cm/1½ in pieces
1.5 litres/2½ pints/6¼ cups chicken
    stock
1 cinnamon stick
good pinch of paprika
pinch of saffron
2 egg yolks
juice of ½ lemon
30ml/2 tbsp chopped fresh coriander
30ml/2 tbsp chopped fresh parsley
150g/5oz vermicelli
salt and freshly ground black pepper
Moroccan bread, to serve

1 Heat the oil and butter in a saucepan or flameproof casserole and fry the onion for 3–4 minutes until softened. Dust the chicken pieces in seasoned flour and fry gently until evenly browned.

2 Transfer the chicken to a plate and add the carrots and parsnip to the pan. Cook over a gentle heat for 3–4 minutes, stirring frequently, then return the chicken to the pan. Add the stock, cinnamon stick and paprika and season well with salt and pepper.

3 Bring the soup to the boil, cover and simmer for 1 hour until the vegetables are very tender.

4 While the soup is cooking, blend the saffron in 30ml/2 tbsp boiling water. Beat the egg yolks with the lemon juice in a separate bowl and add the chopped coriander and parsley. When the saffron water has cooled, stir into the egg and lemon mixture.

5 When the vegetables are tender, transfer the chicken to a plate. Spoon away any excess fat from the soup, then increase the heat a little and stir in the vermicelli. Cook for 5–6 minutes until the noodles are tender.

6 Meanwhile, remove the skin from the chicken and, if liked, bone and chop into bite-size pieces. If you prefer, simply skin the chicken and leave the pieces whole.

7 When the vermicelli is cooked, reduce the heat and stir in the chicken pieces and the egg, lemon and saffron mixture. Cook over a very low heat for 1–2 minutes, stirring all the time. Adjust the seasoning and serve with Moroccan bread.

Sizzling Prawns

For a really tasty starter, fry prawns in a blend of Moroccan spices. It couldn't be simpler.

INGREDIENTS

Serves 4
450g/1lb raw king prawns in
   their shells
30ml/2 tbsp olive oil
25–40g/1–1½oz/2–3 tbsp butter
2 garlic cloves, crushed
5ml/1 tsp ground cumin
2.5ml/½ tsp ground ginger
10ml/2 tsp paprika
1.5ml/½ tsp cayenne pepper
lemon wedges and fresh coriander
   sprigs, to garnish

1 Pull the heads off the prawns and then peel away the shells, legs and tails. Using a sharp knife, cut along the back of each prawn and pull away and discard the dark thread.

2 Heat the olive oil and butter in a frying pan. When the butter begins to sizzle, add the garlic and cook for about 30 seconds.

3 Add the cumin, ginger, paprika and cayenne pepper. Cook briefly, stirring for a few seconds, and then add the prawns. Cook for 2–3 minutes over a high heat, until they turn pink, stirring frequently.

4 Transfer the prawns to four warmed serving dishes and pour the butter and spicy mixture over. Garnish with lemon wedges and coriander and serve immediately.

Grilled Keftas

INGREDIENTS

Makes 12–14
675g/1½lb lamb
1 onion, quartered
3–4 fresh parsley sprigs
2–3 fresh coriander sprigs
1–2 fresh mint sprigs
2.5ml/½ tsp ground cumin
2.5ml/½ tsp mixed spice
5ml/1 tsp paprika
salt and freshly ground black pepper
Moroccan bread, to serve

For the mint dressing
30ml/2 tbsp finely chopped fresh mint
90ml/6 tbsp natural yogurt

1 Roughly chop the lamb, place in a food processor and process until smooth. Transfer to a plate.

2 Add the onion, parsley, coriander and mint to the processor and process until finely chopped. Add the lamb together with the spices and seasoning and process again until very smooth. Transfer to a bowl and chill for about 1 hour.

3 Make the dressing. Blend the chopped fresh mint with the yogurt and chill until required.

4 Mould the meat into small sausage shapes and skewer with wooden or metal kebab sticks. Preheat a grill or barbecue.

5 Cook the keftas for 5–6 minutes, turning once. Serve immediately with the mint dressing. Moroccan bread makes a good accompaniment.

Meat Briouates

The Moroccans, who enjoy the taste of sweet and savoury together, traditionally sprinkle these little pastry snacks with ground cinnamon and icing sugar. It is an unusual but delicious combination.

INGREDIENTS

Makes about 24
175g/6oz filo pastry
40g/1½oz/3 tbsp butter, melted
sunflower oil, for frying
fresh flat leaf parsley, to garnish
ground cinnamon and icing sugar,
  to serve (optional)

For the meat filling
30ml/2 tbsp sunflower oil
1 onion, finely chopped
1 small bunch fresh coriander, chopped
1 small bunch fresh parsley, chopped
375g/12oz lean minced beef or lamb
2.5ml/½ tsp paprika
5ml/1 tsp ground coriander
good pinch of ground ginger
2 eggs, beaten

1 First make the filling. Heat the oil in a frying pan and fry the onion and herbs over a low heat for about 4 minutes until the onion is softened. Add the meat and cook for about 5 minutes, stirring frequently, until the meat is evenly browned and most of the moisture has evaporated.

2 Drain away any excess fat and stir in the spices. Cook for 1 minute, remove the pan from the heat and stir in the beaten eggs. Stir until they begin to set and resemble lightly scrambled eggs. Set aside.

3 Take a sheet of filo pastry and cut into 8.5cm/3½in strips. Cover the remaining pastry with clear film to prevent it drying out. Brush the strip with melted butter, then place a heaped teaspoon of the meat filling at one end of the strip, about 1cm/½in from the end. Fold one corner over the filling to make a triangular shape.

4 Fold the "triangle" over itself and then continue to fold, keeping the triangle shape, until you reach the end of the strip. Continue in this way until all the mixture has been used up. You should make about 24 pastries.

5 Heat about 1cm/½in oil in a heavy-based pan and fry the *briouates* in batches for 2–3 minutes until golden, turning once. Drain on kitchen paper and arrange on a serving plate. Serve garnished with fresh parsley and sprinkled with ground cinnamon and icing sugar, if liked.

Prawn Briouates

In Morocco, *briouates* are made with a special pastry called *ouarka*. Like filo, it is very thin but it is very tricky to make and takes a great deal of practice. Filo makes a good substitute.

INGREDIENTS

Makes about 24
175g/6oz filo pastry
40g/1½oz/3 tbsp butter, melted
sunflower oil, for frying
spring onion and coriander leaves,
    to garnish
ground cinnamon and icing sugar,
    to serve (optional)

For the prawn filling
15ml/1 tbsp olive oil
15g/½oz/1 tbsp butter
2–3 spring onions, finely chopped
15g/½oz/2 tbsp plain flour
300ml/½ pint/1¼ cups milk
2.5ml/½ tsp paprika
350g/12oz cooked peeled
    prawns, chopped
salt and white pepper

1 First make the filling. Heat the olive oil and butter in a saucepan and fry the spring onions over a very gentle heat for 2–3 minutes until soft. Stir in the flour, and then slowly add the milk to make a smooth sauce.

2 Season the sauce with paprika, salt and pepper and stir in the prawns.

3 Take a sheet of filo pastry and cut it in half widthways, to make a rectangle about 18 x 14cm/7 x 5½in. Cover the remaining pastry with clear film to prevent it drying out.

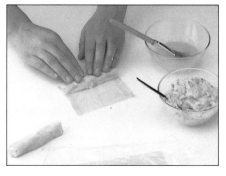

4 Brush the pastry with melted butter and then place a heaped teaspoon of filling at one end of the pastry. Roll up like a cigar, tucking in the sides as you go. Continue in this way until you have used all the filling.

5 Heat about 1cm/½in oil in a heavy-based pan and fry the *briouates*, in batches if necessary, for 2–3 minutes until golden, turning occasionally. Drain on kitchen paper and then serve garnished with a spring onion and coriander leaves, and sprinkled with cinnamon and icing sugar, if liked.

Chakcouka

This is a Moroccan version of a dish from neighbouring Tunisia. Include one or two red or orange peppers as you need the sweetness of the riper fruit.

INGREDIENTS

Serves 4
45ml/3 tbsp olive oil
1 Spanish onion, finely sliced
1 garlic clove, crushed
4 peppers, cored, seeded and sliced
4–5 tomatoes, peeled and chopped
250ml/8fl oz/1 cup puréed canned
   tomatoes or tomato juice
25ml/1½ tbsp chopped fresh parsley
5ml/1 tsp paprika (optional)
a little lemon juice (optional)
4 eggs
45ml/3 tbsp single cream
salt and freshly ground black pepper

1 Preheat the oven to 180°C/350°F/ Gas 4. Heat the oil in a frying pan and gently fry the onion and garlic for about 5 minutes until softened, stirring occasionally.

2 Add the sliced peppers to the pan and fry over a gentle heat for about 10 minutes, stirring occasionally, until softened slightly.

3 Add the chopped tomatoes, the puréed tomatoes or juice, 15ml/ 1 tbsp of the parsley, the paprika, if using, and seasoning and stir well. Cook over a gentle heat for a further 10 minutes until the peppers are fairly soft. Season to taste, and sharpen with lemon juice, if liked.

4 Spoon the mixture into four ovenproof dishes, preferably earthenware. Make a well in the centre and break an egg into each hole. Spoon some of the cream over each egg yolk and sprinkle with a little black pepper or paprika, as liked.

5 Bake for about 15 minutes until the white of the egg is set. Sprinkle with the remaining chopped parsley before serving.

Roasted Aubergines

Aubergines are a favourite Moroccan vegetable. They are often eaten fried or, as here, roasted with spices in a hot oven.

INGREDIENTS

Serves 4
1 large or 2 small aubergines
salt
ground cumin, paprika and cayenne
   pepper, or lemon wedges and mint
   leaves, to serve

For the paprika oil
10ml/2 tsp paprika
60ml/4 tbsp water
60ml/4 tbsp sunflower oil

1 Slice the aubergines lengthways, place in a colander, sprinkle with salt and set aside on a plate for about 30 minutes. Meanwhile, make the paprika oil. Place the paprika, water and oil in a pan, bring to the boil and simmer for 10 minutes. Carefully pour the oil from the surface into a heatproof container, discarding the sediment. Preheat the oven to 190°C/375°F/ Gas 5. Rinse the aubergines and pat dry with kitchen paper.

2 Brush each side of the aubergines generously with the paprika oil and place on a baking tray. Bake for 15–20 minutes until lightly golden.

3 Blend together equal proportions of cumin and paprika and season with cayenne pepper. Serve the aubergine slices warm with the spice mixture, or simply serve with salt and a sprinkling of mint leaves plus lemon wedges for squeezing.

Olives with Moroccan Marinades

INGREDIENTS

Serves 6–8

225g/8oz/1⅓ cups green or tan olives
(unpitted) for each marinade

For the Moroccan marinade
45ml/3 tbsp chopped fresh coriander
45ml/3 tbsp chopped fresh flat
   leaf parsley
1 garlic clove, finely chopped
good pinch of cayenne pepper
good pinch of ground cumin
30–45ml/2–3 tbsp olive oil
30–45ml/2–3 tbsp lemon juice

For the spicy herb marinade
60ml/4 tbsp chopped fresh coriander
60ml/4 tbsp chopped fresh flat
   leaf parsley
1 garlic clove, finely chopped
5ml/1 tsp grated fresh root ginger
1 red chilli, seeded and finely sliced
¼ preserved lemon, cut into thin strips

1 Crack the olives, hard enough to break the flesh, but taking care not to crack the stone. Place in a bowl of cold water and leave overnight to remove the excess brine. Drain thoroughly and place in a jar.

2 Blend the ingredients for the Moroccan marinade and pour over half the olives, adding more olive oil and lemon juice to cover, if necessary.

3 To make the spicy herb marinade, mix together the coriander, parsley, garlic, ginger, chilli and preserved lemon. Add the remaining olives. Store the olives in the fridge for at least 1 week, shaking the jars occasionally.

Byesar

The Arab dish Byesar is similar to Middle Eastern hummus, but uses broad beans instead of chick-peas. In Morocco, it is eaten by dipping bread into ground spices and then scooping up the purée.

INGREDIENTS

Serves 4–6

115g/4oz dried broad beans, soaked
2 garlic cloves, peeled
5ml/1 tsp cumin seeds
about 60ml/4 tbsp olive oil
salt
mint sprigs, to garnish
extra cumin, cayenne pepper and
   bread, to serve

1 Put the dried broad beans in a pan with the whole garlic cloves and cumin seeds and add enough water just to cover. Bring to the boil, then reduce the heat and simmer until the beans are tender. Drain, cool and then slip off the outer skin of each bean.

2 Purée the beans in a blender or food processor, adding sufficient olive oil and water to give a smooth soft dip. Season to taste with plenty of salt. Garnish with sprigs of mint and serve with extra cumin seeds, cayenne pepper and bread.

COUSCOUS
AND TAGINES

Couscous is the national dish of Morocco and is one of the country's most delicious dishes. The term refers both to the grain and to the dish itself, in which the grain is doused in a tasty tagine of fish, meat, poultry or vegetables. Tagine also has two meanings, being either the cooking pot or the stew. Each household has its favourite recipe and it is unlikely to be exactly like its neighbour's.

Monkfish Couscous

Since fish needs very little cooking, it is quickest and easiest to cook the couscous using this simple method. However, if you prefer to steam couscous, steam it over the onions and peppers.

INGREDIENTS

Serves 4

675g/1½lb monkfish
30ml/2 tbsp olive oil
1 onion, very thinly sliced into rings
25g/1oz/3 tbsp raisins
40g/1½oz/¼ cup cashew nuts
1 small red pepper, cored, seeded and sliced
1 small yellow pepper, cored, seeded and sliced
4 tomatoes, peeled, seeded and sliced
350ml/12fl oz/1½ cups fish stock
15ml/1 tbsp chopped fresh parsley
salt and freshly ground black pepper

For the couscous

275g/10oz/1⅔ cups couscous
525ml/18fl oz/2¼ cups boiling vegetable stock or water

1 Bone and skin the monkfish, if necessary, and cut into bite-size chunks using a sharp knife.

2 Heat half the oil in a saucepan or flameproof casserole and fry about a quarter of the onion rings for 5–6 minutes until they are a dark golden brown. Transfer to a plate lined with kitchen paper.

3 Add the raisins and stir-fry for 30–60 seconds until they begin to plump up. Add to the plate with the onion rings. Add the cashew nuts to the pan and stir-fry for 30–60 seconds until golden. Place on the plate with the onion and raisins and set aside.

4 Heat the remaining oil in the pan and add the remaining onion rings. Cook for 4–5 minutes until golden, and then add the pepper slices. Cook over a fairly high heat for 6–8 minutes until the peppers are soft, stirring occasionally. Add the tomatoes and fish stock, reduce the heat and simmer for 10 minutes.

5 Meanwhile, prepare the couscous. Place in a bowl, pour over the boiling stock or water and stir once or twice. Set aside for 10 minutes so that the couscous can absorb the liquid, then fluff up with a fork. Cover and keep warm. Alternatively, prepare according to the instructions on the packet.

6 Add the fish to the peppers and onion, partially cover and simmer for 6–8 minutes until the fish is tender, stirring gently occasionally. Season to taste with salt and pepper.

7 Pile the couscous on to a large serving plate and make a hollow in the middle. Pour over the monkfish and peppers with all the sauce. Sprinkle with the parsley and the reserved onion rings, raisins and cashew nuts and serve.

Seven-vegetable Couscous

Seven is a magical number in Morocco and there are many recipes for this glorious celebration couscous. The vegetables here are carrots, parsnips, turnips, onions, courgettes, tomatoes and French beans. You could substitute different vegetables if you wish.

INGREDIENTS

Serves 6
30ml/2 tbsp sunflower or olive oil
450g/1lb lean lamb, cut into
   bite-size pieces
2 chicken breast quarters, halved
2 onions, chopped
350g/12oz carrots, cut into chunks
225g/8oz parsnips, cut into chunks
115g/4oz turnips, cut into cubes
6 tomatoes, peeled and chopped
900ml/1½ pints/3¾ cups chicken stock
good pinch of ginger
1 cinnamon stick
400g/14oz can chick-peas, drained
400g/14oz/2 cups couscous
2 small courgettes, cut into
   julienne strips
115g/4oz French beans, trimmed and
   halved if necessary
50g/2oz/⅓ cup raisins
a little harissa or Tabasco sauce
salt and freshly ground black pepper

1 Heat half the oil in a large saucepan or flameproof casserole and fry the lamb, in batches if necessary, until evenly browned, stirring frequently. Transfer to a plate with a slotted spoon. Add the chicken pieces and cook until evenly browned. Transfer to the plate with the lamb.

2 Heat the remaining oil and add the onions. Fry over a gentle heat for 2–3 minutes, stirring occasionally, then add the carrots, parsnips and turnips. Stir well, cover with a lid and "sweat" over a gentle heat for 5–6 minutes, stirring once or twice.

3 Add the tomatoes, lamb, chicken and stock. Season with salt and black pepper and add the ginger and cinnamon. Bring to the boil and simmer gently for 35–45 minutes until the meat is nearly tender.

4 Skin the chick-peas by placing them in a bowl of cold water and rubbing them between your fingers. The skins will rise to the surface. Discard the skins and drain. Prepare couscous according to the instructions on the packet.

5 Add the skinned chick-peas, courgettes, beans and raisins to the meat mixture, stir gently and continue cooking for 10–15 minutes until the vegetables and meat are tender. Pile the couscous on to a large serving platter, making a slight well in the centre.

6 Transfer the chicken to a plate and remove the skin and bone, if you wish. Spoon 3–4 large spoonfuls of stock into a separate saucepan. Stir the chicken back into the stew, add harissa or Tabasco sauce to the separate stock and heat both gently. Spoon the stew over the couscous. Serve the harissa sauce in a separate bowl.

Pumpkin Couscous

Pumpkin is a very popular Moroccan ingredient and this is another traditional couscous, with echoes of the very early vegetable couscous dishes made by the Berbers.

Ingredients

Serves 4–6

75g/3oz/½ cup chick-peas, soaked overnight
675g/1½lb lean lamb, cut into bite-size pieces
2 Spanish onions, sliced
pinch of saffron
1.5ml/¼ tsp ground ginger
2.5ml/½ tsp ground turmeric
5ml/1 tsp ground black pepper
450g/1lb carrots
675g/1½lb pumpkin
75g/3oz/⅔ cup raisins
400g/14oz/2 cups couscous
salt
fresh parsley, to garnish

1 Drain the chick-peas and cook in plenty of boiling water for 1–1½ hours until tender. Place in a bowl of cold water and remove the skins by rubbing with your fingers. The skins will float to the surface. Discard the skins and drain.

2 Place the lamb, onions, saffron, ginger, turmeric, pepper, salt and 1.2 litres/2 pints/5 cups water in a *couscousier* or large saucepan. Slowly bring to the boil, then cover and simmer for about 1 hour until the meat is tender.

3 Meanwhile, prepare the vegetables. Peel or scrape the carrots and cut into 6cm/2½in pieces. Cut the pumpkin into 2.5cm/1in cubes, discarding the skin, seeds and pith.

4 Stir the carrots, pumpkin and raisins into the meat mixture, cover the pan and simmer for a further 30–35 minutes until the vegetables and meat are completely tender.

5 Prepare the couscous according to the instructions on the packet.

6 Spoon the couscous on to a large warmed serving plate, making a well in the centre. Spoon the stew and the gravy into the centre, arranging some of the pieces of carrot down the sides of the couscous, or alternatively stir the stew into the couscous. Extra gravy can be poured into a separate jug. Garnish with parsley and serve.

Sea Bass and Fennel Tagine

This is a delicious tagine where the fish is flavoured with *charmoula*, a favourite blend of herbs and spices used especially in fish dishes.

INGREDIENTS

Serves 4
675g/1½lb sea bass, monkfish or
   cod fillets
225g/8oz raw Mediterranean prawns
30ml/2 tbsp olive oil
1 onion, chopped
1 fennel bulb, sliced
225g/8oz small new potatoes, halved
475ml/16fl oz/2 cups fish stock
lemon wedges, to serve (optional)

For the *charmoula*

2 garlic cloves, crushed
20ml/4 tsp ground cumin
20ml/4 tsp paprika
pinch of chilli powder or
   cayenne pepper
30ml/2 tbsp chopped fresh parsley
30ml/2 tbsp chopped fresh coriander
45ml/3 tbsp white vinegar
15ml/1 tbsp lemon juice

1 First make the *charmoula* by blending the crushed garlic, spices, herbs, vinegar and lemon juice together in a bowl.

2 Skin the fish if necessary and remove any bones, then cut into large bite-size chunks. Top and tail the prawns and pull away the shell. Using a sharp knife, cut along the back of each prawn and pull away and discard the dark thread.

3 Place the fish and prawns in two separate shallow dishes, add half the *charmoula* marinade to each dish and stir well to coat evenly. Cover with clear film and set aside in a cool place for 30 minutes–2 hours.

4 Heat the oil in a large flameproof casserole and fry the onion for 2 minutes. Add the sliced fennel and continue cooking over a gentle heat for 5–6 minutes until the onion and fennel are flecked with brown. Add the potatoes and fish stock and cook for a further 10–15 minutes until the potatoes are tender.

5 Add the marinated fish, stir gently and cook for 4 minutes, then add the prawns and all the remaining marinade and cook for a further 5–6 minutes until the fish is tender and the prawns are pink.

6 Serve in bowls, with lemon wedges for squeezing if you wish.

Chicken Kdra with Chick-peas and Almonds

A *kdra* is a type of tagine that is traditionally cooked with *smen*, a strong Moroccan butter, and a lot of onions. The almonds in this recipe are precooked until soft, adding an interesting texture and flavour to the chicken.

INGREDIENTS

Serves 4

75g/3oz/½ cup blanched almonds
75g/3oz /½ cup chick-peas, soaked overnight
4 part-boned chicken breasts, skinned
50g/2oz/4 tbsp butter
2.5ml/½ tsp saffron
2 Spanish onions, finely sliced
900ml/1½ pints/3¾ cups chicken stock
1 small cinnamon stick
60ml/4 tbsp chopped fresh flat leaf parsley, plus extra to garnish
lemon juice, to taste
salt and freshly ground black pepper

1 Place the almonds in a pan of water and simmer for 1½–2 hours until fairly soft, then drain. Cook the chick-peas for 1–1½ hours until soft. Drain the chick-peas, then place in a bowl of cold water and rub with your fingers to remove the skins. Discard the skins and drain.

2 Place the chicken pieces in a pan, together with the butter, half of the saffron, salt and plenty of black pepper. Heat gently, stirring, until the butter has melted.

3 Add the onions and stock, bring to the boil and then add the chick-peas and cinnamon stick. Cover and cook very gently for 45–60 minutes until the chicken is completely tender.

4 Transfer the chicken to a serving plate and keep warm. Bring the sauce to the boil and simmer until well reduced, stirring frequently. Add the almonds, parsley and remaining saffron and cook for a further 2–3 minutes. Sharpen the sauce with a little lemon juice, then pour over the chicken and serve, garnished with extra parsley.

Chicken with Tomatoes and Honey

INGREDIENTS

Serves 4

30ml/2 tbsp sunflower oil
25g/1oz/2 tbsp butter
4 chicken quarters or 1 whole chicken, quartered
1 onion, grated or very finely chopped
1 garlic clove, crushed
5ml/1 tsp ground cinnamon
good pinch of ground ginger
1.5kg/3–3½lb tomatoes, peeled, cored and roughly chopped
30ml/2 tbsp clear honey
50g/2oz/⅓ cup blanched almonds
15ml/1 tbsp sesame seeds
salt and freshly ground black pepper
Moroccan corn bread, to serve

1 Heat the oil and butter in a large casserole. Add the chicken pieces and cook over a medium heat for about 3 minutes until the chicken is lightly browned.

2 Add the onion, garlic, cinnamon, ginger, tomatoes and seasoning, and heat gently until the tomatoes begin to bubble.

3 Lower the heat, cover and simmer very gently for 1 hour, stirring and turning the chicken occasionally, until it is completely cooked through.

4 Transfer the chicken pieces to a plate and then increase the heat and cook the tomatoes until the sauce is reduced to a thick purée, stirring frequently. Stir in the honey, cook for a minute and then return the chicken to the pan and cook for 2–3 minutes to heat through. Dry fry the almonds and sesame seeds or toast under the grill until golden.

5 Transfer the chicken and sauce to a warmed serving dish and sprinkle with the almonds and sesame seeds. Serve with Moroccan corn bread.

Fish with Spinach and Lime

Use fresh spinach for this dish, both for flavour and texture.

INGREDIENTS

Serves 4
675g/1½lb white fish, such as
　haddock, cod, sea bass or monkfish
sunflower oil, for frying
500g/1¼lb potatoes, sliced
1 onion, chopped
1–2 garlic cloves, crushed
5 tomatoes, peeled and chopped
375g/12oz fresh spinach, chopped
lime wedges, to garnish

For the *charmoula*
6 spring onions, chopped
10ml/2 tsp fresh thyme
60ml/4 tbsp chopped flat leaf parsley
30ml/2 tbsp chopped fresh coriander
10ml/2 tsp paprika
generous pinch of cayenne pepper
60ml/4 tbsp olive oil
grated rind of 1 lime and 60ml/4 tbsp
　lime juice
salt

1 Cut the fish into large pieces, discarding any skin and bones, and place in a large shallow dish.

2 Blend together the ingredients for the *charmoula* and season well with salt. Pour over the fish, stir to mix and leave in a cool place, covered with clear film, for 2–4 hours.

3 Heat about 5mm/¼in oil in a large heavy pan and fry the potatoes until cooked through and golden. Drain on kitchen paper.

4 Pour off all but 15ml/1 tbsp of the oil and add the chopped onion, garlic and tomatoes. Cook over a gentle heat for 5–6 minutes, stirring occasionally, until the onion is soft. Place the potatoes on top and then pile the chopped spinach into the pan.

5 Place the fish on top of the spinach and pour over all the marinade. Cover tightly and steam for 15–18 minutes. After about 8 minutes, carefully stir the contents of the pan, so that the fish at the top is distributed throughout the dish. Cover again and continue cooking, but check occasionally – the dish is cooked once the fish is tender and opaque and the spinach has wilted.

6 Serve immediately on individual serving plates, garnished with wedges of lime.

Chicken with Preserved Lemon and Olives

This is one of the most famous Moroccan dishes. You must use preserved lemon as fresh lemon simply doesn't have the mellow flavour that this dish requires. For a truly authentic flavour, use tan-coloured Moroccan olives.

INGREDIENTS

Serves 4

30ml/2 tbsp olive oil
1 Spanish onion, chopped
3 garlic cloves
1cm/½in fresh root ginger, grated, or
  2.5ml/½ tsp ground ginger
2.5–5ml/½–1 tsp ground cinnamon
pinch of saffron
4 chicken quarters, preferably breasts,
  halved if liked
750ml/1¼ pints/3 cups chicken stock
30ml/2 tbsp chopped fresh coriander
30ml/2 tbsp chopped fresh parsley
1 preserved lemon
115g/4oz/⅔ cup Moroccan tan olives
salt and freshly ground black pepper
lemon wedges and fresh coriander
  sprigs, to garnish

1 Heat the oil in a large flameproof casserole and fry the onion for 6–8 minutes over a moderate heat until lightly golden, stirring occasionally.

2 Meanwhile, crush the garlic and blend with the ginger, cinnamon, saffron and a little salt and pepper. Stir into the pan and fry for 1 minute. Add the chicken pieces, in batches if necessary, and fry over a moderate heat for 2–3 minutes until lightly browned.

3 Add the chicken stock, coriander and parsley, bring to the boil and then cover and simmer very gently for 45 minutes until the chicken is tender.

4 Rinse the preserved lemon under cold water, discard the flesh and cut the peel into small pieces. Stir into the pan with the olives and simmer for a further 15 minutes until the chicken is very tender.

5 Transfer the chicken to a plate and keep warm. Bring the sauce to the boil and cook for 3–4 minutes until reduced and fairly thick. Pour over the chicken and serve, garnished with lemon wedges and coriander sprigs.

Lamb Tagine with Artichokes and Preserved Lemon

You can use stewing or braising beef for this tagine if you prefer.

INGREDIENTS

Serves 4–6

675g/1½lb leg of lamb, trimmed and
   cut into cubes
2 onions, very finely chopped
2 garlic cloves, crushed
60ml/4 tbsp chopped fresh parsley
60ml/4 tbsp chopped fresh coriander
good pinch of ground ginger
5ml/1 tsp ground cumin
90ml/6 tbsp olive oil
350–400ml/12–14fl oz/1½–1⅔ cups
   water or stock
1 preserved lemon
400g/14oz can artichoke hearts,
   drained and halved
15ml/1 tbsp chopped fresh mint, plus
   extra sprigs to garnish
1 egg, beaten (optional)
salt and freshly ground black pepper
couscous, to serve

1 Place the meat in a shallow dish. Stir together the onions, garlic, parsley, coriander, ginger, cumin, seasoning and olive oil. Stir into the meat, cover with clear film and set aside to marinate for 3–4 hours or, preferably, overnight.

2 Heat a large heavy-based saucepan and stir in the meat and all the marinade. Cook over a fairly high heat for 5–6 minutes until the meat is evenly brown, then stir in enough water or stock to just cover the meat. Bring to the boil, cover and simmer for 45–60 minutes until the meat is just tender.

3 Rinse the preserved lemon under cold water, discard the flesh and cut the peel into pieces. Stir into the meat and simmer for a further 15 minutes, then add the artichoke hearts and mint.

4 Simmer for a few minutes to warm through. If you wish to thicken the sauce, remove the pan from the heat and stir in some or all of the beaten egg. Garnish with mint and serve with couscous.

Beef Tagine with Sweet Potatoes

This warming dish is eaten during the winter in Morocco, where, especially in the mountains, the weather can be surprisingly cold. Tagines, by definition, are cooked on the hob (or, more often in Morocco, over coals). However, this works well cooked in the oven.

INGREDIENTS

Serves 4
675–900g/1½–2lb braising or
   stewing beef
30ml/2 tbsp sunflower oil
good pinch of ground turmeric
1 large onion, chopped
1 red or green chilli, seeded
   and chopped
7.5ml/1½ tsp paprika
good pinch of cayenne pepper
2.5ml/½ tsp ground cumin
450g/1lb sweet potatoes
15ml/1 tbsp chopped fresh parsley
15ml/1 tbsp chopped fresh coriander
15g/½oz/1 tbsp butter
salt and freshly ground black pepper

1 Trim the meat and cut into 2cm/¾in cubes. Heat the oil in a flameproof casserole and fry the meat, together with the turmeric and seasoning, over a medium heat for 3–4 minutes until evenly brown, stirring frequently.

2 Cover the pan tightly and cook for 15 minutes over a fairly gentle heat, without lifting the lid. Preheat the oven to 180°C/350°F/Gas 4.

3 Add the onion, chilli, paprika, cayenne pepper and cumin to the pan together with just enough water to cover the meat. Cover tightly and cook in the oven for 1–1½ hours until the meat is very tender, checking occasionally and adding a little extra water to keep the stew fairly moist.

4 Meanwhile, peel the sweet potatoes and slice them straight into a bowl of salted water (sweet potatoes discolour very quickly). Transfer to a pan, bring to the boil and then simmer for 2–3 minutes until just tender. Drain.

5 Stir the herbs into the meat, adding a little extra water if the stew appears dry. Arrange the potato slices over the meat and dot with the butter. Cover and cook in the oven for a further 10 minutes or until the potatoes feel very tender. Increase the oven temperature to 200°C/400°F/Gas 6 or heat the grill.

6 Remove the lid of the casserole and cook in the oven or under the grill for a further 5–10 minutes until the potatoes are golden.

FISH AND SEAFOOD

Morocco has a long coast, rich in fish and seafood. The country boasts thousands of wonderful fish recipes as each region tends to have its own traditional dishes. Large fish, like sea bass or sea bream, are cooked whole, either stuffed or baked with vegetables, or with an almond crust, which tastes sublime. Fish is also often marinated in a combination of herbs and spices called charmoula, *which gives a piquant flavour that is quite delicious.*

Sea Bream with Artichokes and Courgettes

INGREDIENTS

Serves 4

1 or 2 whole sea bream or sea bass,
about 1.5kg/3–3½ lb, cleaned and
scaled, with the head and tail left on
2 onions
2–3 courgettes
4 tomatoes
45ml/3 tbsp olive oil
5ml/1 tsp fresh thyme
400g/14oz can artichoke hearts
lemon wedges and finely pared rind,
black olives and fresh coriander
leaves, to garnish

For the *charmoula*

1 onion, chopped
2 garlic cloves, halved
½ bunch fresh parsley
3–4 fresh coriander sprigs
pinch of paprika
45ml/3 tbsp olive oil
30ml/2 tbsp white wine vinegar
15ml/1 tbsp lemon juice
salt and freshly ground black pepper

1 First make the *charmoula*. Place the
ingredients in a food processor with
45ml/3 tbsp water and process until the
onion is finely chopped and the
ingredients are well combined.
Alternatively, chop the onion, garlic
and herbs finely and blend with the
other ingredients and the water.

2 Make three or four slashes on both
sides of the fish. Place in a bowl
and spread with the *charmoula*
marinade, pressing into both sides of
the fish. Set aside for 2–3 hours,
turning the fish occasionally.

3 Slice the onions. Top and tail the
courgettes and cut into julienne
strips. Peel the tomatoes, discard the
seeds and chop roughly.

4 Preheat the oven to 220°C/425°F/
Gas 7. Place the onions, courgettes
and tomatoes in a shallow ovenproof
dish. Sprinkle with the olive oil, salt
and thyme and roast in the oven for
15–20 minutes, until softened and
slightly charred, stirring occasionally.

5 Reduce the oven temperature to
180°C/350°F/Gas 4. Add the
artichokes to the dish and place the
fish, together with the marinade, on
top of the vegetables. Pour over
150ml/¼ pint/⅔ cup water and cover
with foil.

6 Bake for 30–35 minutes or until
the fish is tender. (It will depend
on whether you are cooking 1 large or
2 smaller fish.) For the last 5 minutes of
cooking, remove the foil to allow the
skin to brown lightly. Alternatively,
place under a hot grill for 2–3 minutes.

7 Arrange the fish on a large,
warmed serving platter and spoon
the vegetables around the sides. Garnish
with lemon wedges and finely pared
strips of rind, black olives and fresh
coriander leaves before serving.

Fish Boulettes in Hot Tomato Sauce

This is an unusual and tasty dish that needs scarcely any preparation and produces very little washing up, as it is all cooked in one pan. It serves four people as a main course, but also makes a great starter for eight.

INGREDIENTS

Serves 4

675g/1½lb cod, haddock or
    sea bass fillets
pinch of saffron
½ bunch flat leaf parsley
1 egg
25g/1oz/½ cup white breadcrumbs
25ml/1½ tbsp olive oil
15ml/1 tbsp lemon juice
salt and freshly ground black pepper
fresh flat leaf parsley and lemon
    wedges, to garnish

For the sauce

1 onion, very finely chopped
2 garlic cloves, crushed
6 tomatoes, peeled, seeded and
    chopped
1 green or red chilli, seeded and
    finely sliced
90ml/6 tbsp olive oil
150ml/¼ pint/⅔ cup water
15ml/1 tbsp lemon juice

1 Skin the fish and, if necessary, remove any bones. Cut the fish into large chunks and place in a blender or a food processor.

2 Dissolve the saffron in 30ml/2 tbsp boiling water and pour into the blender or food processor with the parsley, egg, breadcrumbs, olive oil and lemon juice. Season well with salt and pepper and process for 10–20 seconds until the fish is finely chopped and all the ingredients are combined.

3 Mould the mixture into small balls about the size of walnuts and place them in a single layer on a plate.

4 To make the sauce, place the onion, garlic, tomatoes, chilli, olive oil and water in a saucepan. Bring to the boil and then simmer, partially covered, for 10–15 minutes until the sauce is slightly reduced.

5 Add the lemon juice and then place the fish balls in the simmering sauce. Cover and simmer very gently for 12–15 minutes until the fish balls are cooked through, turning them over occasionally.

6 Serve the fish balls and sauce immediately, garnished with flat leaf parsley and lemon wedges.

Moroccan Paella

Spain, particularly Andalucia, has had an important influence on Moroccan cuisine. This dish is especially popular on the coast.

INGREDIENTS

Serves 6

2 large boneless chicken breasts
about 150g/5oz prepared squid
275g/10oz cod or haddock fillets
8–10 raw king prawns, shelled
8 scallops, trimmed and halved
350g/12oz raw mussels in shells
250g/9oz/1⅓ cups long grain rice
30ml/2 tbsp sunflower oil
1 bunch spring onions, cut into strips
2 small courgettes, cut into strips
1 red pepper, cored, seeded and cut
  into strips
400ml/14fl oz/1⅔ cups chicken stock
250ml/8fl oz/1 cup canned
  tomatoes, puréed
salt and freshly ground black pepper
fresh coriander sprigs and lemon
  wedges, to garnish

For the marinade
2 red chillies, seeded
good handful of fresh coriander
10–15ml/2–3 tsp ground cumin
15ml/1 tbsp paprika
2 garlic cloves
45ml/3 tbsp olive oil
60ml/4 tbsp sunflower oil
juice of 1 lemon

1 First make the marinade. Place all the ingredients in a food processor with 5ml/1 tsp salt and process until thoroughly blended.

2 Skin the chicken and cut into bite-size pieces. Place in a glass bowl.

3 Slice the squid into rings. Skin the fish, if necessary, and cut into bite-size chunks. Place the fish and shellfish (apart from the mussels) in a separate glass bowl. Divide the marinade between the fish and chicken and stir well. Cover with clear film and leave to marinate for 2 hours.

4 Scrub the mussels, discarding any that do not close when tapped sharply, and keep in a bowl in the fridge until ready to use. Place the rice in a bowl, cover with boiling water and set aside for about 30 minutes. Drain the chicken and fish, and reserve the marinade separately. Heat the oil in a wok, balti pan or paella pan and fry the chicken pieces for a few minutes until lightly browned.

5 Add the spring onions to the pan, fry for 1 minute and then add the courgettes and red pepper and fry for a further 3–4 minutes until slightly softened. Remove the chicken and then the vegetables to separate plates.

6 Use a spatula to scrape all the marinade into the pan and cook for 1 minute. Drain the rice, add to the pan and stir-fry for 1 minute. Add the chicken stock, puréed tomatoes and reserved chicken, season with salt and pepper and stir well. Bring the mixture to the boil, then cover the pan with a large lid or foil and simmer very gently for 15–20 minutes until the rice is almost tender.

7 Add the reserved vegetables to the pan and place all the fish and mussels on top. Cover again with a lid or foil and cook over a moderate heat for 10–12 minutes until the fish is cooked and the mussels have opened. Discard any mussels that have not opened during the cooking. Serve garnished with fresh coriander and lemon wedges.

Moroccan Tuna Salad

France has had many culinary influences on Moroccan cookery. This salad is similar to the classic *Salade Niçoise* and uses tuna or swordfish steaks and fresh broad beans along with the familiar French beans.

INGREDIENTS

Serves 6
about 900g/2lb fresh tuna or swordfish, sliced into 2cm/³/₄in steaks
olive oil, for brushing

For the salad
450g/1lb French beans
450g/1lb broad beans
1 cos lettuce
450g/1lb cherry tomatoes, halved, unless very tiny
30ml/2 tbsp coarsely chopped fresh coriander
3 hard-boiled eggs
45ml/3 tbsp olive oil
10–15ml/2–3 tsp lime or lemon juice
¹/₂ garlic clove, crushed
175–225g/6–8oz/1¹/₂–2 cups black olives, pitted

For the *charmoula*
1 onion
2 garlic cloves
¹/₂ bunch fresh parsley
¹/₂ bunch fresh coriander
10ml/2 tsp paprika
45ml/3 tbsp olive oil
30ml/2 tbsp white wine vinegar
15ml/1 tbsp lime or lemon juice

1 First make the *charmoula*. Place all the ingredients in a food processor, add 45ml/3 tbsp water and process for 30–40 seconds until finely chopped.

2 Prick the tuna or swordfish steaks all over with a fork, place in a shallow dish and pour over the *charmoula*, turning the fish so that each piece is well coated. Cover with clear film and leave in a cool place for 2–4 hours.

3 To prepare the salad, cook the French beans and broad beans in boiling salted water until tender. Drain and refresh under cold water. Discard the outer shells from the broad beans and place the broad beans in a large serving bowl with the French beans.

4 Discard the outer leaves from the lettuce and tear the inner leaves into pieces. Add to the salad with the tomatoes and coriander. Shell the eggs and cut into eighths. Blend the olive oil, lime or lemon juice and garlic.

5 Preheat the grill and arrange the tuna or swordfish steaks on a grill pan. Brush with the marinade together with a little extra olive oil and grill for 5–6 minutes on each side until the fish is tender and flakes easily. Brush with marinade and more olive oil when turning the fish over.

6 Allow the fish to cool a little and then break the steaks into large pieces. Toss into the salad with the olives and dressing. Decorate with the eggs and serve.

Red Mullet with Cumin

INGREDIENTS

Serves 4
8–12 red mullet, depending on size of
  fish, cleaned, scaled and with heads
  removed if liked
fresh parsley and finely pared strips of
  lemon rind, to garnish

For the *charmoula*
10ml/2 tsp ground cumin
5ml/1 tsp paprika
60ml/4 tbsp lemon juice
45ml/3 tbsp olive oil
30ml/2 tbsp chopped fresh parsley
salt and freshly ground black pepper

For the fresh tomato sauce
5 large tomatoes
2 garlic cloves, chopped
60ml/4 tbsp chopped fresh parsley
  and coriander
30ml/2 tbsp olive oil
30ml/2 tbsp lemon juice

1 Make 2–3 slashes along the sides of
the fish and place in a shallow dish.
Blend together the ingredients for the
charmoula and rub into the fish on both
sides. Set aside for 2 hours.

2 Make the fresh tomato sauce. Peel
the tomatoes and cut into small
pieces, discarding the core and seeds.
Place in a bowl and stir in the
remaining ingredients. Set aside in the
fridge or a cool place.

3 Heat the grill or prepare the
barbecue. Grill or barbecue the fish
for 3–4 minutes on each side, until the
flesh is tender. Garnish with parsley and
lemon rind and serve immediately with
the fresh tomato sauce.

Fish Brochettes

INGREDIENTS

Serves 4 as a starter
450g/1lb white fish fillets, such as cod,
  haddock, monkfish or sea bass
olive oil, for brushing
lime wedges and fresh tomato sauce,
  to serve

For the *charmoula*
$\frac{1}{2}$ onion, grated or very finely chopped
2 garlic cloves, crushed
30ml/2 tbsp chopped fresh coriander
15ml/1 tbsp chopped fresh parsley
5ml/1 tsp ground cumin
10ml/2 tsp paprika
good pinch of ground ginger
25ml/1$\frac{1}{2}$ tbsp white wine vinegar
30ml/2 tbsp lime juice
salt and cayenne pepper

1 First make the *charmoula*. Blend
together all the ingredients and
season to taste with salt and a pinch of
cayenne pepper.

2 Cut the fish into 1cm/$\frac{1}{2}$in cubes,
discarding any skin and bones.
Place in a shallow dish and add the
charmoula, stirring to ensure all the fish
is coated thoroughly. Cover with clear
film and set aside for about 2 hours.

3 Prepare the barbecue or preheat the
grill. Thread the fish on to 12 small
or 8 larger wooden or metal kebab
skewers. Place on a grill pan or on a
rack above the coals and brush with a
little olive oil. Cook the kebabs for
7–10 minutes until the fish is cooked
through, turning and brushing with
more olive oil occasionally. Serve with
wedges of lime and fresh tomato sauce.

--- COOK'S TIP ---

If cooking over coals, use metal skewers or
soak wooden satay sticks in water for an
hour before using. The brochettes may take
less time if barbecuing – it will depend on
the thickness of the fish and the heat and
distance from the coals – so keep a constant
check on them.

Sea Bass with Almond Crust

This is a surprising – and quite delicious – way to cook fish. The almond crust is almost a biscuit, and its sweetness complements the flavour of the sea bass, as well as keeping the fish deliciously moist and succulent.

INGREDIENTS

Serves 4

1 large or 2 small sea bass, about
  1.5kg/3–3½ lb total weight, cleaned
  and scaled, with head and tail left on
15ml/1 tbsp sunflower oil
175g/6oz/1 cup blanched almonds
about 65g/2½ oz/⅓ cup butter,
  softened
2.5–5ml/½–1 tsp ground cinnamon
25g/1oz/¼ cup icing sugar
1 onion, finely sliced
good pinch of saffron
salt and freshly ground black pepper
lime wedges and sprigs of fresh flat leaf
  parsley, to garnish

1 Rinse the fish in cold running water and pat dry.

2 Heat the oil in a small frying pan and fry the almonds for 2–3 minutes over a brisk heat until golden, stirring frequently. Drain on absorbent paper until cool and then grind in a spice or coffee mill.

3 Pour the ground almonds into a bowl or food processor and blend with 25g/1oz/2 tbsp of the butter, the cinnamon, icing sugar and 60ml/4 tbsp water to make a smooth paste.

4 Preheat the oven to 190°C/375°F/ Gas 5. Butter an ovenproof dish, large enough to take the whole fish, with about 15g/½ oz/1 tbsp of the butter. Scatter the sliced onion in the dish. Dissolve the saffron in 15ml/ 1 tbsp boiling water and add to the dish with some salt and pepper.

5 Stuff the fish with half of the almond mixture and place it on top of the onion. Using a spatula, spread the remaining almond paste evenly over the top of the fish.

6 Melt the remaining butter, pour over the fish and then bake in the oven, uncovered, for 45–50 minutes (35–40 minutes if you are cooking 2 smaller fish) until the fish flakes easily and the almond topping is crusty.

7 Transfer the fish to a warmed serving plate and arrange the onion slices and any biscuit topping around the edge. Garnish with lime wedges and flat leaf parsley and serve.

Monkfish with Tomatoes and Olives

This makes a really delicious lunch or light supper dish. Alternatively, serve as a starter for six to eight people.

INGREDIENTS

Serves 4

8 tomatoes
675g/1½lb monkfish
30ml/2 tbsp plain flour
5ml/1 tsp ground coriander
2.5ml/½ tsp ground turmeric
25g/1oz/2 tbsp butter
2 garlic cloves, finely chopped
15–30ml/1–2 tbsp olive oil
40g/1½oz/4 tbsp pine nuts, toasted
small pieces of preserved lemon
12 black olives, pitted
salt and freshly ground black pepper
whole slices of preserved lemon and
   chopped fresh parsley, to garnish

1 Peel the tomatoes by placing them briefly in boiling water, then cold water. Quarter them, remove the cores and seeds and chop roughly.

2 Cut the fish into bite-size chunks. Blend together the flour, coriander, turmeric and seasoning. Dust the fish with the seasoned flour and set aside.

3 Melt the butter in a medium non-stick frying pan and fry the tomatoes and garlic over a gentle heat for 6–8 minutes until the tomatoes are very thick and most of the liquid has evaporated.

4 Push the tomatoes to the edge of the frying pan, moisten the pan with a little olive oil and fry the monkfish pieces in a single layer over a moderate heat for 3–5 minutes, turning frequently. You may have to do this in batches, so as the first batch of fish pieces cooks, place them on top of the tomatoes and fry the remaining fish, adding a little more olive oil to the pan, if necessary.

5 When all the fish is cooked, add the pine nuts and stir, scraping the bottom of the pan to remove the glazed tomatoes. The sauce should be thick and slightly charred in places.

6 Rinse the preserved lemon in cold water, discard the pulp and cut the peel into strips. Stir into the sauce with the olives, adjust the seasoning and serve garnished with whole slices of preserved lemon and parsley.

MEAT AND POULTRY

M'choui, *Moroccan roast lamb, in which a whole lamb is roasted over charcoal, is one of the oldest and most famous Moroccan meat dishes. Lamb is used in tagines, couscous, keftas, stuffings and brochettes. It is almost always cooked until melt-in-the-mouth tender. Like lamb, poultry is rubbed with pungent spices and herbs, and basted throughout with meat juices so that it is always well-flavoured and deliciously moist.*

Moroccan Roast Chicken

In Morocco, a whole chicken is commonly cooked on a spit over hot charcoal. However, it is still excellent roasted in a hot oven and can be cooked whole, halved or in quarters.

INGREDIENTS

Serves 4-6

1.75kg/4−4½lb chicken
2 small shallots
1 garlic clove
1 fresh parsley sprig
1 fresh coriander sprig
5ml/1 tsp salt
7.5ml/1½ tsp paprika
pinch of cayenne pepper
5−7.5ml/1−1½ tsp ground cumin
about 40g/1½oz/3 tbsp butter
½−1 lemon (optional)
sprigs of fresh parsley or coriander, to garnish

1 Remove the chicken giblets if necessary and rinse out the cavity with cold running water. Unless cooking it whole, cut the chicken in half or into quarters using poultry shears or a sharp knife.

2 Place the shallots, garlic, herbs, salt and spices in a food processor or blender and process until the shallots are finely chopped. Add the butter and process to make a smooth paste.

3 Thoroughly rub the paste over the skin of the chicken and then allow it to stand for 1−2 hours.

4 Preheat the oven to 200°C/400°F/Gas 6 and place the chicken in a roasting tin. If using, quarter the lemon and place one or two quarters around the chicken pieces (or in the body cavity if the chicken is whole) and squeeze a little juice over the skin. Roast in the oven for 1−1¼ hours (2−2¼ hours for a whole bird) until the chicken is cooked through and the meat juices run clear. Baste occasionally during cooking with the juices in the roasting tin. If the skin browns too quickly, cover the chicken loosely with foil or greaseproof paper.

5 Allow the chicken to stand for 5−10 minutes, covered in foil, before carving, and then serve garnished with sprigs of fresh parsley or coriander.

Pan-fried Chicken

The essence of this dish is to cook it quickly over a fierce heat, and it therefore works best with small quantities as larger amounts would have less contact with the pan and would tend to braise rather than fry. Served with bread, this dish makes an excellent first course, in which case it will serve four. If you wish to serve four as a main course, double the quantities and either cook in batches or use two pans.

INGREDIENTS

Serves 2 as a main course, 4 as a starter
2 skinned and boned chicken breasts
1 small red or green chilli, seeded and
   finely sliced
2 garlic cloves, finely sliced
3 spring onions, sliced
4–5 wafer-thin slices fresh root ginger
2.5ml/½ tsp ground coriander
2.5ml/½ tsp ground cumin
30ml/2 tbsp olive oil
25ml/1½ tbsp lemon juice
30ml/2 tbsp pine nuts
15ml/1 tbsp raisins (optional)
oil, for frying
15ml/1 tbsp chopped fresh coriander
15ml/1 tbsp chopped fresh mint
salt and freshly ground black pepper
sprigs of fresh mint and lemon wedges,
   to garnish
bread, rice or couscous, to serve

1 Cut the chicken breasts horizontally into three or four thin slices: this will speed up cooking. Place in a shallow bowl.

2 Blend together the chilli, garlic, spring onions, spices, olive oil, lemon juice, pine nuts and raisins, if using. Season with salt and pepper and then pour over the chicken pieces, stirring so that each piece is coated. Cover with clear film and leave in a cool place for 1–2 hours.

3 Brush a wok, balti pan or cast iron frying pan with oil and heat. Add the chicken slices and stir-fry over a fairly high heat for 3–4 minutes until the chicken is browned on both sides.

4 Add the remaining marinade and continue to cook over a high heat for 6–8 minutes until the chicken is browned and cooked through. (The timing will depend on the thickness of the chicken, but make sure that it is completely cooked.)

5 Reduce the heat and stir in the coriander and mint. Cook for 1 minute and serve immediately, garnished with mint sprigs and lemon wedges. Serve with bread as a starter or, if preferred, with rice or couscous as a main course.

Poussins with Courgettes and Apricot Stuffing

If possible, buy very small or baby poussins for this recipe. If these are not available, buy slightly larger poussins and serve half per person.

INGREDIENTS

Serves 4
4 small poussins
about 40g/1½oz/3 tbsp butter
5–10ml/1–2 tsp ground coriander
1 large red pepper
1 red chilli
15–30ml/1–2 tbsp olive oil
120ml/4fl oz/½ cup chicken stock
30ml/2 tbsp cornflour
salt and freshly ground black pepper
fresh flat leaf parsley, to garnish

For the stuffing

525ml/18fl oz/2¼ cups chicken or
    vegetable stock
275g/10oz/1⅔ cups couscous
2 small courgettes
8 ready-to-eat dried apricots
15ml/1 tbsp chopped fresh flat
    leaf parsley
15ml/1 tbsp chopped fresh coriander
juice of ½ lemon

1 First make the stuffing. Bring the stock to the boil and pour it over the couscous in a large bowl. Stir once and then set aside for 10 minutes.

2 Meanwhile, top and tail the courgettes and then grate coarsely. Roughly chop the apricots and add to the courgettes. Preheat the oven to 200°C/400°F/Gas 6.

3 When the couscous has swollen, fluff up with a fork and then spoon 90ml/6 tbsp into a separate bowl and add the courgettes and chopped apricots. Add the herbs, seasoning and lemon juice and stir to make a fairly loose stuffing. Set aside the remaining couscous for serving.

4 Spoon the stuffing loosely into the body cavities of the poussins and secure with string or cocktail sticks. Place the birds in a medium or large roasting tin so that they fit comfortably but not too closely. Rub the butter into the skins and sprinkle with ground coriander and a little salt and pepper.

COOK'S TIP

You can reheat the couscous in two ways: either cover the bowl with clear film and microwave on High for 2–3 minutes, stirring once or twice, or place in a colander or steamer and set over a pan of simmering water. If liked, finely chopped herbs can be added to the couscous to give colour.

5 Cut the red pepper into medium-sized strips and finely slice the chilli, discarding the seeds and core. Place in the roasting tin around the poussins and spoon over the olive oil.

6 Roast in the oven for 20 minutes, then reduce the oven temperature to 180°C/350°F/Gas 4. Pour the stock around the poussins and baste each with the stock and red pepper/chilli mixture. Return the tin to the oven and cook for a further 30–35 minutes until the poussins are cooked through and the meat juices run clear, basting occasionally with the stock.

7 When the poussins are cooked, transfer to a warmed serving plate. Blend the cornflour with 45ml/3 tbsp cold water, stir into the stock and peppers in the roasting tin and heat gently, stirring all the time, until the sauce is slightly thickened. Taste, and adjust the seasoning, and then pour into a jug or pour over the poussins. Garnish the birds with fresh flat leaf parsley and serve at once with the reserved couscous.

Bisteeya

Bisteeya is one of the most elaborate and intriguing dishes in Moroccan cuisine. It is the centrepiece at feasts and banquets, and is normally made using pigeon, which is then layered with wafer-thin pastry and cooked in a tin over hot coals. This is a considerably simplified version, using chicken instead of pigeon and filo pastry instead of the traditional – but very tricky to make – *ouarka*. Nevertheless, you and your guests will be delighted with this delicious and unusual dish.

INGREDIENTS

Serves 4
30ml/2 tbsp sunflower oil, plus extra
   for brushing
25g/1oz/2 tbsp butter
3 chicken quarters, preferably breasts
1½ Spanish onions, grated or very
   finely chopped
good pinch of ginger
good pinch of saffron
10ml/2 tsp ground cinnamon, plus
   extra for dusting
40g/1½oz/4 tbsp flaked almonds
1 large bunch fresh coriander,
   finely chopped
1 large bunch fresh parsley,
   finely chopped
3 eggs, beaten
about 175g/6oz filo pastry
5–10ml/1–2 tsp icing sugar (optional),
   plus extra for dusting
salt and freshly ground black pepper

1 Heat the oil and butter in a large flameproof casserole or saucepan and brown the chicken pieces for about 4 minutes. Add the grated onions, the ginger, saffron, 2.5ml/½ tsp of the cinnamon and enough water so that the chicken braises, rather than boils (about 300ml/½ pint/1¼ cups). Season well with salt and pepper.

2 Bring to the boil and then cover and simmer very gently for 45–55 minutes or until the chicken is tender and completely cooked. Meanwhile, dry fry the almonds until golden and set aside.

3 Transfer the chicken to a plate and, when cool enough to handle, remove the skin and bones and cut the flesh into pieces.

4 Stir the coriander and parsley into the pan and simmer the sauce until well reduced and thick. Add the beaten eggs and cook over a very gentle heat until the eggs are lightly scrambled.

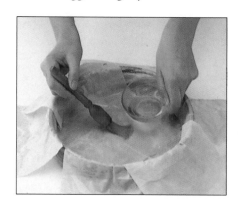

5 Preheat the oven to 180°C/350°F/ Gas 4. Oil a shallow round ovenproof dish, about 25cm/10in in diameter. Place one or two sheets of filo pastry in a single layer over the bottom of the dish (it will depend on the size of your filo pastry), so that it is completely covered and the edges of the pastry sheets hang over the sides. Brush lightly with oil and make two more layers of filo, brushing with oil between the layers.

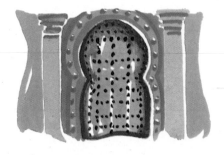

6 Place the chicken on the pastry and then spoon the egg and herb mixture on top.

7 Place a single layer of filo pastry on top of the filling (you may need to use more than one sheet of filo pastry) and scatter with the almonds. Sprinkle with the remaining cinnamon and the icing sugar, if using.

8 Fold the edges of the filo over the almonds and then make four further layers of filo (using one or two sheets per layer, depending on size), brushing each layer with a little oil. Tuck the filo edges under the pie (as if you were making a bed!) and brush the top layer with oil.

9 Bake in the oven for 40–45 minutes until golden. Dust the top with icing sugar and use the extra cinnamon to make criss-cross or diagonal lines. Serve immediately.

Roast Chicken with Almonds

INGREDIENTS

Serves 4

1.5kg/3–3½ lb chicken
pinch of ground ginger
pinch of ground cinnamon
pinch of saffron, dissolved in
   30ml/2 tbsp boiling water
2 onions, chopped
300ml/½ pint/1¼ cups chicken stock
45ml/3 tbsp flaked almonds
15ml/1 tbsp plain flour
salt and freshly ground black pepper
lemon wedges and coriander to garnish

For the stuffing

50g/2oz/⅓ cup couscous
120ml/4fl oz/½ cup chicken stock
20g/¾oz/1½ tbsp butter
1 shallot, finely chopped
½ small cooking apple
25ml/1½ tbsp flaked almonds
30ml/2 tbsp ground almonds
30ml/2 tbsp chopped fresh coriander
good pinch of paprika
pinch of cayenne pepper

1 Preheat the oven to 180°C/350°F/ Gas 4. Prepare the stuffing. Place the couscous in a bowl, bring the chicken stock to the boil and pour it over the couscous. Stir with a fork and then set aside for 10 minutes for the couscous to swell. Meanwhile, melt the butter in a small frying pan and fry the shallot for 2–3 minutes until soft.

2 Fluff up the couscous and stir in the shallot and all the butter from the pan. Peel, core and chop the apple and add to the couscous with the remaining stuffing ingredients. Season with salt and pepper and stir well.

3 Loosely push the couscous mixture into the neck end of the chicken and truss the chicken neatly or secure the neck with cocktail sticks.

4 Blend the ginger and cinnamon with the saffron water. Rub the chicken with salt and pepper and then pour over the saffron water.

5 Place the chicken in a small roasting tin or dish so that it fits snugly. Spoon the chopped onions and stock around the edge and then cover the dish with foil, pinching the foil around the edges of the dish firmly so that the chicken sits in a foil "tent".

6 Cook for 1¼ hours and then increase the oven temperature to 200°C/400°F/Gas 6. Transfer the chicken to a plate and strain the cooking liquid into a jug, reserving the onions. Place the chicken back in the roasting tin with the onions, baste with a little of the cooking liquid and scatter with the flaked almonds.

7 Return to the oven and cook for about 30 minutes until the chicken is golden brown and cooked through.

8 Pour off the fat from the reserved cooking juices and pour into a small saucepan. Blend the flour with 30ml/2 tbsp cold water, stir into the pan with the cooking juices and heat gently, stirring to make a smooth sauce. Garnish the chicken with lemon wedges and coriander and serve with the sauce.

Grilled Spatchcocked Poussins

These little chickens can be cooked under the grill, but taste best if cooked, Moroccan-style, over charcoal.

INGREDIENTS

Serves 4
2 large or 4 small poussins
green salad, to serve

For the marinade
150ml/¼ pint/⅔ cup olive oil
1 onion, grated
1 garlic clove, crushed
15ml/1 tbsp chopped fresh mint
15ml/1 tbsp chopped fresh flat
   leaf parsley
15ml/1 tbsp chopped fresh coriander
5–10ml/1–2 tsp ground cumin
5ml/1 tsp paprika
pinch of cayenne pepper

1 Tuck the wings of each poussin under the body and remove the wishbone. Turn the birds over and cut along each side of the backbone with poultry shears and remove.

2 Push down on each bird to break the breast bone. Keeping the bird flat, push a skewer through the wings and breast. Push another skewer through the thighs.

3 Blend together all the marinade ingredients and spread over both sides of the poussins. Place in a large shallow dish, cover with clear film and marinate for at least 4 hours or overnight.

4 Prepare a barbecue or preheat the grill. Barbecue the poussins for about 25–35 minutes, turning occasionally and brushing with the marinade. If grilling, cook under a medium grill about 7.5cm/3in from the heat for 25–35 minutes or until cooked through, turning and basting occasionally.

5 When ready to serve, cut the birds in half. Serve with a green salad.

Moroccan Rabbit

The subtle spices make the perfect accompaniments to rabbit.

INGREDIENTS

Serves 4
675g/1½lb prepared rabbit pieces
pinch of saffron
1 garlic clove, crushed
pinch of ground turmeric
5ml/1 tsp paprika
good pinch of ground cumin
1 onion, grated
25g/1oz/2 tbsp butter
15ml/1 tbsp finely chopped fresh
   coriander
50g/2oz/scant ½ cup raisins
5ml/1 tsp garam masala or mixed spice
salt and freshly ground black pepper
30ml/2 tbsp flaked almonds, toasted,
   to garnish

1 Preheat the oven to 180°C/350°F/ Gas 4 and place the rabbit pieces in a casserole.

2 Blend together the saffron and 30ml/2 tbsp boiling water and stir to dissolve. Add the garlic, turmeric, paprika, cumin and salt and pepper and rub this mixture into the rabbit pieces.

3 Add the onion, half the butter, the coriander and 600ml/1 pint/ 2½ cups boiling water. Cover and cook in the oven for 50 minutes, then transfer the rabbit pieces to a shallow heatproof dish and rub with the remaining butter.

4 Increase the oven temperature to 190°C/375°F/Gas 5. Cook the rabbit pieces for 8–10 minutes until browned and place on a serving plate.

5 Meanwhile, pour the sauce into a small saucepan, add the raisins and garam masala or mixed spice and simmer until reduced by about half. Pour the sauce over the rabbit and garnish with the flaked almonds.

Moroccan-style Roast Lamb

Lamb is by far the most favoured meat of Morocco, where whole or half lambs are still cooked over open fires. In this oven-roasted variation of *M'choui* the meat is cooked in a very hot oven to start and then finished in a cooler oven until it is so tender that it falls from the bone.

INGREDIENTS

Serves 6
1.5kg/3–3½lb leg of lamb
40g/1½oz/3 tbsp butter
2 garlic cloves, crushed
2.5ml/½ tsp cumin seeds
1.5ml/¼ tsp paprika
pinch of cayenne pepper
salt
fresh coriander, to garnish
bread or roast potatoes, to serve

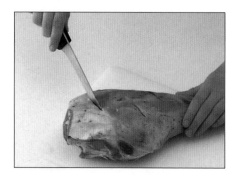

1 Trim the lamb of excess fat and make several shallow diagonal cuts over the meat.

2 Blend together the butter, garlic, cumin, paprika, cayenne pepper and salt and spread over the surface of the lamb, pressing the mixture into the slits. Set aside for at least 2 hours or overnight.

3 Preheat the oven to 220°C/425°F/ Gas 7. Place the meat in a large roasting tin and cook for 15 minutes. (Be warned: the butter will burn, but the resulting flavour is delicious.) Reduce the oven temperature to 180°C/350°F/Gas 4 and continue cooking for 1½–2 hours, until the meat is well cooked and very tender, basting several times with the meat juices.

4 Place the cooked meat on a serving plate and serve immediately. In Morocco, it is customary to pull the meat away from the bone using a fork; however, it may be carved if you prefer. Garnish with fresh coriander and serve Moroccan-style with bread, or with roast potatoes.

Shish Kebab

This is one of the most famous dishes of the Arab world, commonly served with spices – cumin, cayenne pepper and salt – and invariably with Moroccan bread. Lamb is the traditional Moroccan meat for this dish, although beef can be used and is more popular in the French-speaking parts of the country.

INGREDIENTS

Serves 4
675g/1½lb lamb or beef
1 onion, grated
30ml/2 tbsp chopped fresh parsley
5ml/1 tsp paprika
5ml/1 tsp ground cumin
15ml/1 tbsp olive oil
15ml/1 tbsp lemon juice
salt and freshly ground black pepper
lemon wedges and parings to garnish
Moroccan bread, ground cumin and
    cayenne pepper, to serve

1 Cut the meat into fairly small pieces, measuring approximately 2cm/¾in square.

COOK'S TIP

Moroccan cooks often intersperse lamb or beef fat with the meat, which adds flavour and keeps the meat moist. Alternatively, if using lamb, choose a more fatty cut, like shoulder or fillet, where the fat is marbled through the flesh.

2 Mix the grated onion, most of the parsley, paprika, cumin, oil, lemon juice and seasoning in a bowl and add the meat. Stir so that the meat is coated thoroughly and set aside for about 2 hours.

3 Prepare a barbecue or preheat the grill. Thread the meat on to metal skewers, allowing about 6–8 pieces of meat per skewer.

4 Grill or barbecue the meat a few centimetres from the heat for 6–8 minutes or until it is cooked through, basting occasionally with the marinade.

5 Arrange the kebabs on a serving plate and garnish with the remaining parsley, lemon wedges and parings. Serve with Moroccan bread and dishes of cumin, cayenne pepper and salt.

Moroccan Stuffed Leg of Lamb

Moroccans always serve meat very well cooked. If you prefer lamb slightly pink, reduce the cooking time a little.

INGREDIENTS

Serves 6

1.5kg/3–3½ lb leg of lamb, boned
2 garlic cloves, crushed
40g/1½oz/3 tbsp butter
175ml/6fl oz/¾ cup chicken stock
15ml/1 tbsp cornflour
15ml/1 tbsp apricot jam
salt and freshly ground black pepper

For the stuffing

1 green chilli, seeded
2 shallots
1 garlic clove
1 bunch fresh coriander
sprig of fresh parsley
25g/1oz/2 tbsp butter
10ml/2 tsp ground cumin
2.5ml/½ tsp ground cinnamon
150g/5oz/¾ cup cooked long
   grain rice
30ml/2 tbsp pine nuts

3 Place the cooked rice in a bowl, add the pine nuts and then stir in the contents of the pan. Season well with salt and pepper.

5 Place in a roasting tin and cook in the oven for 20 minutes, then reduce the heat to 180°C/350°F/Gas 4 and continue to roast for 1½–2 hours, basting occasionally with the juices from the tin.

1 Preheat the oven to 200°C/400°F/Gas 6 and then make the stuffing. Place the seeded chilli, whole shallots, garlic clove, coriander and parsley in a food processor and process until very finely chopped.

2 Melt the butter in a small frying pan and fry the shallot and herb mixture for 2–3 minutes over a gentle heat to soften the shallots. Add the cumin and cinnamon and stir well.

4 Season the meat on both sides with salt and pepper and rub the outside with the crushed garlic and butter. Place the meat, skin side down, on a work surface and spread the stuffing evenly over it. Roll the meat up, secure with a skewer and then tie with cooking string at even intervals.

6 To make the sauce, pour away the excess fat from the roasting tin and then add the chicken stock. Heat gently, stirring all the time, to deglaze the tin. Blend the cornflour with 30ml/2 tbsp water and add to the roasting tin with the apricot jam. Gradually bring to the boil, stirring all the time. Strain the sauce into a serving jug and serve with the stuffed lamb.

VEGETABLES AND SIDE DISHES

Anyone who visits a Moroccan market will be struck by the fabulous stalls of fresh fruit and vegetables. Vegetables feature in many tagines and couscous dishes and are also popular in their own right, in salads and side dishes. These, like Black and Orange Salad and Tagine of Onions, are eaten as snacks in the morning, while more substantial dishes are served for lunch or as part of an evening meal.

Spinach and Chick-pea Pancakes

In this Moroccan-style dish spinach and courgettes are combined with chick-peas and wrapped in light pancakes.

INGREDIENTS

Serves 4–6
15ml/1 tbsp olive oil
1 large onion, chopped
250g/9oz fresh spinach
400g/14oz can chick-peas, drained
2 courgettes, grated
30ml/2 tbsp chopped fresh coriander
2 eggs, beaten
salt and freshly ground black pepper
fresh coriander leaves, to garnish

For the pancake batter
150g/5oz/1¼ cups plain flour
1 egg
about 350ml/12fl oz/1½ cups milk
15ml/1 tbsp sunflower or olive oil
butter or oil, for greasing

For the sauce
25g/1oz/2 tbsp butter
30ml/2 tbsp plain flour
about 300ml/½ pint/1¼ cups milk

1 First make the pancakes. Blend together the flour, a little salt, the egg, milk and 75ml/5 tbsp water to make a fairly thin batter. Stir in the oil.

2 Heat a large griddle, grease lightly and fry the pancakes on one side only, to make eight large pancakes. Set aside while preparing the filling.

3 Heat the oil in a small frying pan and fry the onion for 4–5 minutes until soft, stirring occasionally. Wash the spinach, place in a pan and cook until wilted, shaking the pan occasionally. Chop the spinach roughly.

4 Skin the chick-peas: place them in a bowl of cold water and rub them until the skins float to the surface. Mash the skinned chick-peas roughly with a fork. Add the onion, grated courgettes, spinach and coriander. Stir in the beaten eggs, season and mix well.

5 Place the pancakes, cooked side up, on a work surface and place spoonfuls of filling down the centre. Fold one half of each pancake over the filling and roll up. Place in a large buttered ovenproof dish and preheat the oven to 180°C/350°F/Gas 4.

6 Melt the butter for the sauce in a small saucepan, stir in the flour and then gradually add the milk to make a smooth sauce. Season with salt and pepper and pour over the pancakes.

7 Bake in the oven for about 15 minutes until golden and serve garnished with coriander leaves.

Schlada

This is the Moroccan cousin of gazpacho – indeed the word gazpacho is Arabic in origin, meaning soaked bread. The Spaniards learned of gazpacho from the Moors, who made it with garlic, bread, olive oil and lemon juice. Tomatoes and peppers were introduced later, after Columbus returned from America with these new world fruits, and this version of the dish in turn made its way back to North Africa.

INGREDIENTS

Serves 4
3 green peppers, quartered
4 large tomatoes
2 garlic cloves, finely chopped
30ml/2 tbsp olive oil
30ml/2 tbsp lemon juice
good pinch of paprika
pinch of ground cumin
1/4 preserved lemon
salt and freshly ground black pepper
fresh coriander and flat leaf parsley,
    to garnish

1 Grill the peppers skin side up until the skins are blackened, place in a plastic bag and tie the ends. Leave for about 10 minutes until the peppers are cool enough to handle and peel away the skins.

2 Cut the peppers into small pieces, discarding the seeds and core, and place in a serving dish.

3 Peel the tomatoes by placing in boiling water for 1 minute, then plunging into cold water. Peel off the skins, then quarter them, discarding the core and seeds. Chop roughly and add to the peppers. Scatter the chopped garlic on top and chill for 1 hour.

4 Blend together the olive oil, lemon juice, paprika and cumin and pour over the salad. Season with salt and pepper.

5 Rinse the preserved lemon in cold water and remove the flesh and pith. Cut the peel into slivers and sprinkle over the salad. Garnish with coriander and flat leaf parsley.

Cauliflower with Tomatoes and Cumin

This makes an excellent side dish to serve with barbecued meat or fish.

INGREDIENTS

Serves 4
30ml/2 tbsp sunflower or olive oil
1 onion, chopped
1 garlic clove, crushed
1 small cauliflower, broken into florets
5ml/1 tsp cumin seeds
a good pinch of ground ginger
4 tomatoes, peeled, seeded
 and quartered
15–30ml/1–2 tbsp lemon juice
 (optional)
30ml/2 tbsp chopped fresh coriander
 (optional)

1 Heat the oil in a cast iron pan, add the onion and garlic and stir-fry for 2–3 minutes until the onion is softened. Add the cauliflower and stir-fry for a further 2–3 minutes until the cauliflower is flecked with brown. Add the cumin seeds and ginger, fry briskly for 1 minute, and then add the tomatoes, 175ml/6fl oz/³/₄ cup water and some salt and pepper.

2 Bring to the boil and then reduce the heat, cover with a plate or with foil and simmer for 6–7 minutes, until the cauliflower is just tender.

3 Stir in a little lemon juice to sharpen the flavour, if liked, and adjust the seasoning if necessary. Scatter over the chopped coriander, if using, and serve at once.

Roast Vegetable Salad

Oven roasting brings out all the flavours of these classic Mediterranean vegetables. Serve them hot with meat or fish.

INGREDIENTS

Serves 4
2–3 courgettes
1 Spanish onion
2 red peppers
16 cherry tomatoes
2 garlic cloves, chopped
pinch of cumin seeds
5ml/1 tsp fresh thyme or 4–5 torn
 basil leaves
60ml/4 tbsp olive oil
juice of ½ lemon
5–10ml/1–2 tsp harissa or
 Tabasco sauce
fresh thyme sprigs, to garnish

1 Preheat the oven to 220°C/425°F/ Gas 7. Top and tail the courgettes and cut into long strips. Cut the onion into thin wedges. Cut the peppers into chunks, discarding the seeds and core.

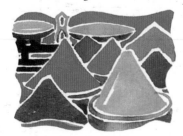

2 Place the vegetables in a cast iron dish or roasting tin, add the tomatoes, chopped garlic, cumin seeds and thyme or basil. Sprinkle with the olive oil and toss to coat. Cook in the oven for 25–30 minutes until the vegetables are very soft and slightly charred at the edges.

3 Blend the lemon juice with the harissa or Tabasco sauce and stir into the vegetables before serving, garnished with the thyme.

Couscous Salad

Couscous salad is popular almost everywhere nowadays. In Morocco, as you would expect, there are many ways of serving couscous – this salad has a delicate flavour and is excellent with grilled chicken or kebabs.

INGREDIENTS

Serves 4

275g/10oz/1²/₃ cups couscous
525ml/18fl oz/2¹/₄ cups boiling
  vegetable stock
16–20 black olives
2 small courgettes
25g/1oz/¹/₄ cup flaked almonds, toasted
60ml/4 tbsp olive oil
15ml/1 tbsp lemon juice
15ml/1 tbsp chopped fresh coriander
15ml/1 tbsp chopped fresh parsley
good pinch of ground cumin
good pinch of cayenne pepper
salt

1 Place the couscous in a bowl and pour over the boiling stock. Stir with a fork and then set aside for 10 minutes for the stock to be absorbed. Fluff up with a fork.

— COOK'S TIP —

If preferred, you can reconstitute the pre-cooked couscous by steaming it.

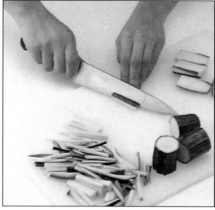

2 Halve the olives, discarding the stones. Top and tail the courgettes and cut into small julienne strips.

3 Carefully mix the courgettes, olives and almonds into the couscous.

4 Blend together the olive oil, lemon juice, herbs, spices and a pinch of salt and stir into the salad.

Chick-pea Tagine

INGREDIENTS

Serves 4–6

150g/5oz/³⁄₄ cup chick-peas, soaked
   overnight, or 2 x 400g/14oz cans
   chick-peas, drained
30ml/2 tbsp sunflower oil
1 large onion, chopped
1 garlic clove, crushed (optional)
400g/14oz can chopped tomatoes
5ml/1 tsp ground cumin
350ml/12fl oz/1½ cups chicken or
   vegetable stock
¼ preserved lemon
30ml/2 tbsp chopped fresh coriander

1 If using dried chick-peas, cook in plenty of boiling water for 1–1½ hours until tender. Drain.

2 Skin the chick-peas by placing them in a bowl of cold water and rubbing them between your fingers – the skins will rise to the surface.

3 Heat the oil in a saucepan or flameproof casserole and fry the onion and garlic, if using, for 8–10 minutes until golden.

4 Add the chick-peas, tomatoes, cumin and stock and stir well. Bring to the boil and simmer, uncovered, for 30–40 minutes, until the chick-peas are very soft and most of the liquid has evaporated.

5 Rinse the preserved lemon and cut away the flesh and pith. Cut the peel into slivers and stir into the chick-peas along with the coriander. Serve immediately with Moroccan bread.

Moroccan-style Broad Beans

Peeling the broad beans is a bit time-consuming, but well worth the effort, and this dish is so delicious that you won't want to eat broad beans any other way.

INGREDIENTS

Serves 4

375g/12oz frozen broad beans
15g/½oz/1 tbsp butter
4–5 spring onions, sliced
15ml/1 tbsp chopped fresh coriander
5ml/1 tsp chopped fresh mint
2.5–5ml/½–1 tsp ground cumin
10ml/2 tsp olive oil
salt

1 Simmer the broad beans in water for 3–4 minutes until tender. Drain and, when cool enough to handle, peel away the outer skin, so you are left with the bright green seed.

2 Melt the butter in a small pan and gently fry the spring onions for 2–3 minutes. Add the broad beans and then stir in the coriander, mint, cumin and a pinch of salt. Stir in the olive oil and serve immediately.

Courgettes with Moroccan Spices

This is a delicious way of cooking courgettes and goes equally well with a Moroccan or Western-style meal.

INGREDIENTS

Serves 4

500g/1¼lb courgettes
lemon juice and chopped fresh
    coriander and parsley, to serve

For the spicy *charmoula*

1 onion
1–2 garlic cloves, crushed
¼ red or green chilli, seeded and
    finely sliced
2.5ml/½ tsp paprika
2.5ml/½ tsp ground cumin
45ml/3 tbsp olive oil
salt and freshly ground black pepper

COOK'S TIP

Buy young courgettes with tender skin –
older courgettes may need to be peeled.

1 Preheat the oven to 180°C/350°F/ Gas 4. Cut the courgettes into quarters or eighths lengthways, depending on their size, and place in a shallow ovenproof dish or casserole.

2 Finely chop or grate the onion and blend with the other *charmoula* ingredients and 60ml/4 tbsp water. Pour over the courgettes. Cover with foil and cook in the oven for about 15 minutes.

3 Baste the courgettes with the *charmoula*, and return to the oven, uncovered, for 5–10 minutes until they are tender. Sprinkle with lemon juice and fresh herbs and serve.

Okra and Tomato Tagine

A spicy vegetarian dish that is delicious served either with other vegetable dishes or as a side dish to accompany a meat tagine.

INGREDIENTS

Serves 4
350g/12oz okra
5–6 tomatoes
2 small onions
2 garlic cloves, crushed
1 green chilli, seeded
5ml/1 tsp paprika
small handful of fresh coriander
30ml/2 tbsp sunflower oil
juice of 1 lemon

1 Trim the okra and then cut into 1cm/½in lengths. Peel and seed the tomatoes and chop roughly.

2 Roughly chop one of the onions and place in a food processor or blender with the garlic, chilli, paprika, coriander and 60ml/4 tbsp water. Blend to a paste.

3 Thinly slice the second onion and fry in the oil for 5–6 minutes until golden brown. Transfer to a plate with a slotted spoon.

4 Reduce the heat and pour in the onion and coriander mixture. Cook for 1–2 minutes, stirring frequently, and then add the okra, tomatoes, lemon juice and about 120ml/4fl oz/½ cup water. Stir well to mix, cover tightly and simmer over a low heat for about 15 minutes until the okra is tender.

5 Transfer to a serving dish, sprinkle with the fried onion rings and serve immediately.

Tagine of Onions

This is a typically sweet dish, flavoured with ground cinnamon, that is much appreciated in Morocco. A Moroccan cook might add three or four times the amount of cinnamon and twice the amount of sugar, but if you're unsure about such sweet flavours with onions, follow this recipe, which uses less than the normal Moroccan quantities.

INGREDIENTS

Serves 4

675g/1½lb Spanish or red onions
90ml/6 tbsp olive or sunflower oil or
 a mixture of both
pinch of saffron
2.5ml/½ tsp ground ginger
5ml/1 tsp ground black pepper
5ml/1 tsp ground cinnamon
15ml/1 tbsp sugar

1 Slice the onions very thinly and place in a shallow dish.

2 Blend together the olive or sunflower oil, saffron, ginger, black pepper, cinnamon and sugar and pour over the onions. Stir gently to mix and then set aside for 2 hours.

3 Preheat the oven to 160°C/325°F/ Gas 3 and pour the onions and the marinade into an ovenproof dish or casserole.

4 Fold a piece of foil into three and place over the top of the dish or casserole, securing with a lid.

5 Cook in the oven for 45 minutes or until the onions are very soft. Increase the oven temperature to 200°C/400°F/Gas 6, remove the lid and foil and cook for 5–10 minutes more until the onions are lightly glazed. Serve with grilled meats.

Black and Orange Salad

This dramatic salad is typically Moroccan – the dark black olives contrasting with oranges, a favourite Moroccan fruit.

INGREDIENTS

Serves 4
3 oranges
115g/4oz/1 cup black olives, pitted
15ml/1 tbsp chopped fresh coriander
15ml/1 tbsp chopped fresh parsley
30ml/2 tbsp olive oil
15ml/1 tbsp lemon juice
2.5ml/½ tsp paprika
2.5ml/½ tsp ground cumin

1 Cut away the peel and pith from the oranges and cut into wedges.

2 Place the oranges in a salad bowl and add the black olives, coriander and parsley.

3 Blend together the olive oil, lemon juice, paprika and cumin. Pour the dressing over the salad and toss gently. Chill for about 30 minutes and serve.

Rocket and Coriander Salad

Rocket leaves have a wonderful, peppery flavour and, mixed with coriander, make a favourite Moroccan salad. However, unless you grow your own rocket, or have a plentiful supply, you may well have to use extra spinach or another green leaf in order to pad this salad out.

INGREDIENTS

Serves 4
115g/4oz or more rocket leaves
115g/4oz young spinach leaves
1 large bunch (about 25g/1oz) fresh coriander
2–3 fresh parsley sprigs
1 garlic clove, crushed
45ml/3 tbsp olive oil
10ml/2 tsp white wine vinegar
pinch of paprika
salt
cayenne pepper

1 Wash the rocket and spinach leaves and place in a salad bowl. Chop the coriander and parsley and add.

2 In a small jug, blend together the garlic, olive oil, vinegar, paprika, salt and cayenne pepper.

3 Pour the dressing over the salad and serve immediately.

Carrot and Orange Salad

This is a wonderful fresh-tasting salad with such a fabulous combination of fruit and vegetables that it is difficult to know whether it is a salad or a dessert. The Moroccans would have no such problem as they would eat it by itself at mid-day with a glass of mint tea.

INGREDIENTS

Serves 4
450g/1lb carrots
2 large oranges
15ml/1 tbsp olive oil
30ml/2 tbsp lemon juice
pinch of sugar (optional)
30ml/2 tbsp chopped pistachio nuts or
   toasted pine nuts
salt and freshly ground black pepper

1 Peel the carrots and grate them into a large bowl.

2 Peel the oranges with a sharp knife and cut into segments, catching the juice in a small bowl.

3 Blend together the olive oil, lemon juice and any orange juice. Season with a little salt and pepper to taste, and sugar if liked.

4 Toss the oranges with the carrots and pour the dressing over. Scatter over the pistachio nuts or pine nuts before serving.

Spinach with Beans, Raisins and Pine Nuts

This dish is traditionally made with chick-peas, but can be made with haricot beans as here. Use either dried or canned beans.

INGREDIENTS

Serves 4

115g/4oz/scant ¾ cup haricot beans,
  soaked overnight, or 400g/14oz
  can, drained
60ml/4 tbsp olive oil
1 thick slice white bread
1 onion, chopped
3–4 tomatoes, peeled, seeded
  and chopped
2.5ml/½ tsp ground cumin
450g/1lb spinach
5ml/1 tsp paprika
1 garlic clove, halved
25g/1oz/3 tbsp raisins
25g/1oz/¼ cup pine nuts, toasted
salt and freshly ground black pepper
Moroccan bread, to serve

1 Cook dried beans in boiling water for about 1 hour until tender. Drain.

2 Heat 30ml/2 tbsp of the oil in a frying pan and fry the bread until golden. Transfer to a plate.

3 Fry the onion in a further 15ml/ 1 tbsp of the oil over a gentle heat until soft but not brown, then add the tomatoes and cumin and continue cooking over a gentle heat.

4 Wash the spinach thoroughly, removing any tough stalks. Heat the remaining oil in a large pan, stir in the paprika and then add the spinach and 45ml/3 tbsp water. Cover and cook for a few minutes until the spinach has wilted.

5 Add the onion and tomato mixture to the spinach and stir in the beans, then season with salt and pepper.

6 Place the garlic and fried bread in a food processor and blend until smooth. Stir into the spinach and bean mixture, together with the raisins. Add 175ml/6fl oz/¾ cup water and then cover and simmer very gently for 20–30 minutes, adding more water if necessary.

7 Place the spinach on a warmed serving plate and scatter with toasted pine nuts. Serve hot with Moroccan bread.

BREADS AND BAKING

Bread is an essential part of a Moroccan meal, eaten as a food and used as an implement for holding meat and vegetables and soaking up gravy. Moroccan bread is made daily in every household and for special occasions, Holiday Bread or Little Spiced Breads, are often baked, too. Moroccans also enjoy a whole range of pastries. Most famous of the cakes is M'Hanncha, Moroccan Serpent Cake, made with ouarka *(or filo pastry) and filled with almonds and sugar.*

Moroccan Bread

Warm this bread in the oven and cut it into thick slices to serve with any classic Moroccan savoury dish – just the thing for mopping up a really tasty sauce.

INGREDIENTS

Makes 2 loaves
275g/10oz/2½ cups strong white flour
175g/6oz/1½ cups wholemeal flour
10ml/2 tsp salt
about 250ml/8fl oz/1 cup warm milk
  and water mixed
10ml/2 tsp sesame seeds

For the yeast starter
150ml/¼ pint/⅔ cup warm milk and
  water mixed
5ml/1 tsp sugar
10ml/2 tsp dried yeast

1 First prepare the yeast. Place the warm milk mixture in a small bowl or jug, stir in the sugar and then sprinkle with the yeast. Stir, then set aside in a warm place for about 10 minutes until the yeast is frothy.

2 In a large bowl, mix together the two flours and salt. Add the yeast mixture and enough warm milk and water to make a fairly soft dough. Knead the mixture into a ball and then knead on a floured work surface for 10–12 minutes until the dough is firm and elastic.

3 Break the dough into two pieces and shape into flattened ball shapes. Place on floured baking trays and press down with your hand to make round breads about 13–15cm/5–6in diameter.

4 Cover the breads with oiled clear film or a clean, damp cloth and set aside for 1–1½ hours in a warm place until risen. The breads are ready to bake when the dough springs back if gently pressed with a finger.

5 Preheat the oven to 200°C/400°F/ Gas 6. Sprinkle the loaves with the sesame seeds and bake for 12 minutes. Reduce the oven temperature to 150°C/300°F/Gas 2 and continue baking the loaves for 20–30 minutes until they are golden brown and sound hollow if tapped.

Holiday Bread

This bread is often made on special occasions – not just holidays, but for birthdays, weddings, or for one of the many religious festivals.

INGREDIENTS

Makes 2 loaves
375g/12oz/3 cups strong white flour
115g/4oz/1 cup corn meal
10ml/2 tsp salt
150ml/¼ pint/⅔ cup warm milk and
    water mixed
25ml/1½ tbsp pumpkin seeds
25ml/1½ tbsp sunflower seeds
15ml/1 tbsp sesame seeds

For the yeast starter
150ml/¼ pint/⅔ cup warm water
5ml/1 tsp sugar
10ml/2 tsp dried yeast

1 First prepare the yeast. Place the warm water in a small bowl or jug, stir in the sugar and then sprinkle with the yeast. Stir once or twice, then set aside in a warm place for about 10 minutes until the yeast is frothy.

2 In a large bowl, mix together the flour, corn meal and salt. Add the yeast mixture and enough of the warm milk and water mixture to make a fairly soft dough. Knead the mixture into a ball and then knead on a floured work surface for about 5 minutes.

3 Add the seeds and knead into the dough. Continue kneading for about 5–6 minutes until the dough is firm and elastic.

4 Break the dough into two pieces and shape into balls, flattening to make a frisbee shape. Place on floured baking trays and press down with your hand to make round breads about 13–15cm/5–6in in diameter.

5 Cover with oiled clear film or a damp cloth and set aside for 1–1½ hours in a warm place until risen. The bread is ready to bake when it springs back if gently pressed with a finger.

6 Preheat the oven to 200°C/400°F/ Gas 6 and bake the breads in the oven for 12 minutes. Reduce the oven temperature to 150°C/300°F/Gas 2 and continue cooking for 20–30 minutes until the loaves are golden and sound hollow if tapped.

Marrakesh Pizza

In Morocco, cooks tend to place flavourings inside rather than on top of the bread. The result is surprising – and very delicious.

INGREDIENTS

Makes 4 pizzas

5ml/1 tsp sugar
10ml/2 tsp dried yeast
450g/1lb/4 cups white flour (or a mixture of white and wholemeal flour, according to preference)
10ml/2 tsp salt
melted butter, for brushing
rocket salad and black olives, to serve

For the filling

1 small onion, very finely chopped
2 tomatoes, peeled, seeded and chopped
25ml/1½ tbsp chopped fresh parsley
25ml/1½ tbsp chopped fresh coriander
5ml/1 tsp paprika
5ml/1 tsp ground cumin
50g/2oz vegetable suet, finely chopped
40g/1½ oz Cheddar cheese, grated

1 First prepare the yeast. Place 150ml/¼ pint/⅔ cup warm water in a small bowl or jug, stir in the sugar and then sprinkle with the yeast. Stir once or twice, then set aside in a warm place for about 10 minutes until the yeast is frothy.

2 Meanwhile, make the filling: Mix together the onion, tomatoes, parsley, coriander, paprika, cumin, suet and cheese, then season with salt and set aside.

3 In a large bowl, mix together the flour and 10ml/2 tsp salt. Add the yeast mixture and enough warm water to make a fairly soft dough (about 250ml/8fl oz/1 cup). Knead the mixture into a ball and then knead on a floured work surface for 10–12 minutes until the dough is firm and elastic.

4 Break the dough into four pieces and roll each into a rectangle, measuring 20 x 30cm/8 x 12in. Spread the filling down the centre of each rectangle, then fold into three, to make a rectangle 20 x 10cm/8 x 4in.

5 Roll out the dough again, until it is the same size as before and again fold into three to make a smaller rectangle. (The filling will be squeezed out in places, but don't worry – just push it back inside the dough.)

6 Place the pizzas on a buttered baking sheet, cover with oiled clear film and leave in a warm place for about 1 hour until slightly risen.

7 Heat a griddle and brush with butter. Prick the pizzas with a fork five or six times on both sides and then fry for about 8 minutes on each side until crisp and golden. Serve immediately, with a little melted butter if liked, and accompanied by rocket salad and black olives.

Little Spiced Breads

These rich breads are delicious served with butter and honey.

INGREDIENTS

Makes 12

5ml/1 tsp sugar
10ml/2 tsp dried yeast
75g/3oz/6 tbsp butter, melted
15ml/1 tbsp orange flower water or
    almond essence (optional)
400g/14oz/3½ cups strong white flour
75g/3oz/¾ cup icing sugar
5ml/1 tsp salt
30ml/2 tbsp sesame seeds
15ml/1 tbsp fennel seeds
1 egg, beaten with 15ml/1 tbsp water

1 First start the yeast. Place 120ml/
4fl oz/½ cup warm water in a jug,
stir in the sugar and sprinkle the yeast
on top. Stir and then set aside for about
10 minutes until frothy.

2 Place the melted butter, orange
flower water or almond essence, if
using, and about 175ml/6fl oz/¾ cup
warm water in a separate jug and stir to
mix. Stir the flour, icing sugar, salt,
sesame seeds and fennel seeds together
in the bowl of a food processor or
blender fitted with the dough blade.

3 Add the yeast and half of the butter
and water mixture to the flour and
process so that they slowly combine.
Continue processing, adding the
remaining butter and water to make a
smooth and glossy dough. (You may
need to add extra flour/warm water.)

4 Continue processing for 1–2
minutes, then transfer the dough to
a floured board and knead by hand for
a few minutes until the dough is
smooth and elastic.

5 Place in a clean, lightly oiled bowl,
cover with clear film and leave in a
warm place for 1–1½ hours until
doubled in size. Knead again for a few
minutes and then break into 12 small
balls and flatten slightly with oiled
hands. Place on a greased baking tray,
cover with oiled clear film and leave to
rise for 1 hour.

6 Preheat the oven to 190°C/375°F/
Gas 5. Brush the breads with
beaten egg and then bake in the oven
for 12–15 minutes or until golden
brown. Serve warm or cold.

Macaroons

Called *Ghoriba* in Morocco, these crisp almond biscuits are a favourite mid-morning snack.

INGREDIENTS

Makes about 30
2 egg yolks
1 egg white
200g/7oz/1¾ cups icing sugar, plus extra for dusting
10ml/2 tsp baking powder
grated rind of ½ lemon
a few drops of vanilla essence
about 350g/12oz/3 cups ground almonds
sunflower oil, for greasing

1 Preheat the oven to 180°C/350°F/ Gas 4. Beat together the egg yolks and egg white with the icing sugar. Add the baking powder, lemon rind and vanilla essence, with enough of the ground almonds to make a stiff paste.

2 Knead the mixture together with your hands. Oil your hands with sunflower oil. Take walnut-sized pieces of paste and roll into small balls. Flatten on a board dusted with icing sugar and then place on a greased baking tray about 4cm/1½in apart. Bake for 15 minutes until golden. Cool on a wire rack.

Honeycomb Pancakes

It is the attractive presentation which makes these simple pancakes, or *Beghrir,* look special. Arrange the cooked pancakes in a honeycomb pattern, before serving with butter, warm honey and perhaps a few dates.

INGREDIENTS

Makes about 12
175g/6oz/1½ cups self-raising flour
10ml/2 tsp baking powder
30ml/2 tbsp caster sugar
1 egg
175ml/6fl oz/¾ cup semi-skimmed milk
15ml/1 tbsp rose or orange flower water
15ml/1 tbsp melted butter
oil, for greasing

1 Mix together the flour, baking powder and sugar. Add the egg and milk and blend to make a thick batter. Stir in the rose or orange flower water and then beat in the melted butter.

2 Heat a frying pan and brush the surface with a little oil. Pour in a small ladleful of batter, smoothing with the back of the spoon to make a round about 10cm/4in across. Cook for a few minutes until bubbles appear on the surface, then place on a large plate.

3 Cook the remaining pancakes in the same way and place them on the plate in overlapping circles to make a honeycomb pattern. Serve warm.

Briouates with Almonds and Dates

It is worth investing in a good-quality honey to dip these delicious pastries into – it makes all the difference.

INGREDIENTS

Makes about 30

15ml/1 tbsp sunflower oil
225g/8oz/1⅓ cups blanched almonds
115g/4oz/⅔ cup stoned dates
25g/1oz/2 tbsp butter (softened)
5ml/1 tsp ground cinnamon
1.5ml/¼ tsp almond essence
40g/1½oz/⅓ cup icing sugar
30ml/2 tbsp orange flower water or rose water
10 sheets of filo pastry
50g/2oz/4 tbsp melted butter
120ml/4fl oz/½ cup fragrant honey
dates, to serve (optional)

1 Heat the oil in a small pan and fry the almonds for a few minutes until golden, stirring all the time. Drain on absorbent paper to cool, then grind in a coffee or spice mill. Pound the dates by hand or process in a blender or a food processor.

2 Spoon the ground almonds into a mixing bowl or into the blender or food processor with the dates and blend with the butter, cinnamon, almond essence, icing sugar and a little orange flower or rose water to taste. If the mixture feels stiff, work in a little extra flower water.

3 Preheat the oven to 180°C/350°F/ Gas 4. Brush a sheet of filo pastry with melted butter and cut into three equal strips, keeping the remaining sheets covered with clear film to prevent them drying out.

4 Place a walnut-sized piece of almond paste at the bottom of each strip. Fold one corner over the filling to make a triangle and then fold up, in triangles, to make a neat package. Brush again with a little butter. Repeat steps 3 and 4 to make about 30 pastries.

5 Place the pastries on a buttered baking sheet and bake for 30 minutes until golden. If possible, cook in batches, as once cooked they are immediately immersed in the honey.

6 While the *briouates* are cooking, pour the honey and a little orange flower or rose water into a saucepan and heat very gently. When the pastries are cooked, lower them one by one into the pan and turn them in the honey so that they are thoroughly coated. Transfer to a plate and cool a little before serving, with dates if you wish.

DESSERTS

Moroccans do not often end a meal with a dessert, they prefer to serve fresh fruit and nuts. However, they love sweet things, and dishes that we would call desserts, like rice pudding and Apricots Stuffed with Almond Paste, are taken with mint tea at any time during the day. Fresh fruit desserts, such as Fresh Fruit Salad or Orange and Date Salad, may be served at the end of a meal and are an excellent foil to a rich tagine or couscous.

Fragrant Rice

Rice puddings are very popular all over Morocco, served either sprinkled with nuts and honey or wrapped in a variety of pastries.

INGREDIENTS

Serves 4
75g/3oz/½ cup short-grain rice
about 900ml/1½ pints/3¾ cups milk
30ml/2 tbsp ground rice
50g/2oz/¼ cup caster sugar
40g/1½oz/⅓ cup ground almonds
5ml/1 tsp vanilla essence
2.5ml/½ tsp almond essence
a little orange flower water (optional)
30ml/2 tbsp chopped dates
30ml/2 tbsp pistachio nuts, finely chopped
30ml/2 tbsp flaked almonds, toasted

1 Place the rice in a saucepan with 750ml/1¼ pints/3 cups of the milk and gradually heat until simmering. Cook, uncovered, over a very low heat for 30–40 minutes, until the rice is completely tender, stirring frequently and adding more milk if necessary.

COOK'S TIP

Orange flower water is used in surprisingly large quantities in Moroccan sweets and pastries. However, unless you are partial to the strongly perfumed flavour, add it very sparingly, taste, then add more as required.

2 Blend the ground rice with the remaining milk and stir into the rice pudding. Slowly bring back to the boil and cook for 1 minute. Stir in the sugar, ground almonds, vanilla and almond essence and orange flower water, if using, and cook until the pudding is thick and creamy. Pour into serving bowls and sprinkle with the chopped dates, pistachios and almonds.

Orange and Date Salad

This is simplicity itself, yet is wonderfully fresh-tasting and essentially Moroccan.

INGREDIENTS

Serves 4–6
6 oranges
15-30ml/1-2 tbsp orange flower water or rose water (optional)
lemon juice (optional)
115g/4oz/⅔ cup stoned dates
50g/2oz/⅓ cup pistachio nuts
icing sugar, to taste
a few toasted almonds

COOK'S TIP

Use fresh dates, if you can, although dried dates are delicious in this salad, too.

1 Peel the oranges with a sharp knife, removing all the pith, and cut into segments, catching the juice in a bowl. Place in a serving dish.

2 Stir in the juice from the bowl together with a little orange flower or rose water, if using, and sharpen with lemon juice, if liked.

3 Chop the dates and pistachio nuts and sprinkle over the salad with a little icing sugar. Chill for 1 hour.

4 Just before serving, sprinkle over the toasted almonds and a little extra icing sugar and serve.

Gazelles' Horns

Kaab el Ghzal is one of Morocco's favourite and best known pastries – so popular that the French have honoured it with its own name, *cornes de gazelles*. The horn-shaped, filled pastries are commonly served at wedding ceremonies.

INGREDIENTS

Makes about 16

200g/7oz/1¾ cups plain flour
25g/1oz/2 tbsp melted butter
about 30ml/2 tbsp orange flower water
   or water
1 large egg yolk, beaten
pinch of salt
icing sugar, to serve

For the almond paste

200g/7oz/scant 2 cups ground almonds
115g/4oz/1 cup icing sugar or
   caster sugar
30ml/2 tbsp orange-flower water
25g/1oz/2 tbsp melted butter
2 egg yolks, beaten
2.5ml/½ tsp ground cinnamon

1 First make the almond paste. Mix together all the ingredients to make a smooth paste.

2 To make the pastry, mix the flour and a little salt and then stir in the melted butter, orange flower water or water, and about three-quarters of the egg yolk. Stir in cold water, little by little, to make a fairly soft dough.

3 Knead the dough for about 10 minutes until smooth and elastic, then place on a floured surface and roll out as thinly as possible. Cut the dough into long strips about 7.5cm/3in wide.

4 Preheat the oven to 180°C/350°F/ Gas 4. Take small pieces of the almond paste and roll them between your hands into thin "sausages" about 7.5cm/3in long with tapering ends.

5 Place these in a line along one side of the strips of pastry, about 3cm/1¼in apart. Dampen the pastry edges with water and then the fold the other half of the strip over the filling and press the edges together firmly.

6 Using a pastry wheel, cut around each "sausage" (as you would with ravioli) to make a crescent shape. Make sure that the edges are firmly pinched together.

7 Prick the crescents with a fork or a needle and place on a buttered baking tray. Brush with the remaining beaten egg yolk and bake for 12–16 minutes until lightly coloured. Cool and then dust with icing sugar.

Apricots stuffed with Almond Paste

Almonds, whether whole, flaked or ground, are a favourite Moroccan ingredient. They have a delightful affinity with apricots and this is a popular – and delicious – dessert.

INGREDIENTS

Serves 6

75g/3oz/scant ½ cup caster sugar
30ml/2 tbsp lemon juice
115g/4oz/1 cup ground almonds
50g/2oz/½ cup icing sugar or caster sugar
a little orange flower water (optional)
25g/1oz/2 tbsp melted butter
2.5ml/½ tsp almond essence
900g/2lb fresh apricots
fresh mint sprigs, to decorate

1 Preheat the oven to 180°C/350°F/ Gas 4. Place the sugar, lemon juice and 300ml/½ pint/1¼ cups water in a small saucepan and bring to the boil, stirring occasionally until the sugar has dissolved. Simmer gently for 5–10 minutes to make a thin sugar syrup.

2 Blend together the ground almonds, icing sugar, orange flower water, if using, butter and almond essence to make a smooth paste.

3 Wash the apricots and then make a slit in the flesh and ease out the stone. Take small pieces of the almond paste, roll into balls and press one into each of the apricots.

4 Arrange the stuffed apricots in a shallow ovenproof dish and carefully pour the sugar syrup around them. Cover with foil and bake in the oven for 25–30 minutes.

5 Serve the apricots with a little of the syrup, if liked, and decorated with sprigs of mint.

Fresh Fruit Salad

When peaches and strawberries are out of season, use bananas and grapes, or any other fruits.

INGREDIENTS

Serves 6
2 eating apples
2 oranges
2 peaches
16–20 strawberries
30ml/2 tbsp lemon juice
15–30ml/1–2 tbsp orange flower
  water
icing sugar, to taste
a few fresh mint leaves, to decorate

1 Peel and core the apples and cut into thin slices. Peel the oranges with a sharp knife, removing all the pith, and segment them, catching any juice in a bowl.

2 Blanch the peaches for 1 minute in boiling water, then peel away the skin and cut the flesh into thick slices. Discard the stone. Hull the strawberries and halve or quarter if large. Place all the fruit in a large serving bowl.

3 Blend together the lemon juice, orange flower water and any orange juice. Taste and add a little icing sugar to sweeten, if liked. Pour the fruit juice mixture over the salad and serve decorated with mint leaves.

COOK'S TIP

There are no rules with this fruit salad, and you could use almost any fruit that you like. Oranges, however, should form the base and apples give a contrast in texture.

Dried Fruit Salad

This is a wonderful combination of fresh and dried fruit and makes an excellent dessert throughout the year. Use frozen raspberries or blackberries in winter.

INGREDIENTS

Serves 4
115g/4oz/½ cup dried apricots
115g/4oz/½ cup dried peaches
1 fresh pear
1 fresh apple
1 fresh orange
115g/4oz/²⁄₃ cup mixed raspberries
  and blackberries
1 cinnamon stick
50g/2oz/¼ cup caster sugar
15ml/1 tbsp clear honey
30ml/2 tbsp lemon juice

1 Soak the apricots and peaches in water for 1–2 hours until plump, then drain and halve or quarter.

2 Peel and core the pear and apple and cut into cubes. Peel the orange with a sharp knife, removing all the pith, and cut into wedges. Place all the fruit in a large saucepan with the raspberries and blackberries.

3 Add 600ml/1 pint/2½ cups water, the cinnamon, sugar and honey and bring to the boil. Cover and simmer very gently for 10–12 minutes, then remove the pan from the heat. Stir in the lemon juice. Allow to cool, then pour into a bowl and chill for 1–2 hours before serving.

Figs and Pears in Honey

A stunningly simple dessert which uses two Moroccan favourites – fresh figs and pears.

INGREDIENTS

Serves 4

1 lemon
90ml/6 tbsp clear honey
1 cinnamon stick
1 cardamom pod
2 pears
8 fresh figs, halved

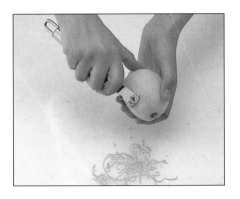

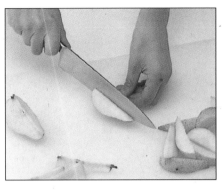

1 Pare the rind from the lemon using a zester or vegetable peeler and cut into very thin strips.

2 Place the lemon rind, honey, cinnamon stick, cardamom pod and 350ml/12fl oz/1½ cups water in a pan and boil, uncovered, for about 10 minutes until reduced by about half.

3 Cut the pears into eighths, discarding the core. Leave the peel on or discard as preferred. Place in the syrup, add the figs and simmer for about 5 minutes until the fruit is tender.

4 Transfer the fruit to a serving bowl. Continue cooking the liquid until syrupy, then discard the cinnamon stick and pour over the figs and pears.

Moroccan-style Cherry Batter Pudding

In France, a batter pudding called clafouti is thickened with flour and eggs. This is a Moroccan version, where ground rice and almonds are used to thicken a more Arab-type milk mixture.

INGREDIENTS

Serves 4

450g/1lb cherries or other fruit
   (see Cook's Tip)
600ml/1 pint/2½ cups skimmed or
   semi-skimmed milk
45ml/3 tbsp ground rice
30–45ml/2–3 tbsp caster sugar
75g/3oz/¾ cup flaked almonds
30ml/2 tbsp orange flower water or
   rose water, to taste

1 Preheat the oven to 190°C/375°F/ Gas 5. Stone the cherries or prepare other fruit appropriately.

2 Bring the milk to the boil. Blend the ground rice with 30–45ml/ 2–3 tbsp cold water, beating well to remove lumps. Pour the milk over the blended rice and then pour back into the pan and simmer over a low heat for 5 minutes until the mixture thickens, stirring all the time.

3 Add the sugar and flaked almonds and cook gently for a further 5 minutes, then stir in the orange flower or rose water and simmer for about 2 minutes more.

4 Butter a shallow ovenproof dish and pour in the almond milk mixture. Arrange the fruit on top and bake for about 25–30 minutes until the fruit has softened. Dust with icing sugar and serve.

> **COOK'S TIP**
>
> Cherries taste delicious in this clafouti but if out of season, almost any fruit, such as apricots, peaches, plums or greengages, can be used. Remove the stones from the fruit and, for apples or pears, peel if liked.

Index